JASAMINE HILL, MA.ED

HOW TO TURN

YOUR FEAR INTO FUEL, YOUR PASSION

INTO YOUR PURPOSE, AND ENJOY THE RIDE OF LIFE

ISBN: 9781795598378

Interior Design: B.O.Y. Enterprises, Inc.

Printed in the United States.

DEDICATION

Grandma Hill, Uncle Robert, and Latongia
Your spirits are always with me.
Thank you.
My guardian angels.

TABLE OF CONTENTS

INTRODUCTION   1

CHAPTER 1   DÉJÀ VU   12

CHAPTER 2   PREPARE FOR THE JOURNEY   36

CHAPTER 3   YOU SCARED, HUH?   73

CHAPTER 4   THE MAP OF THE PARK   95

CHAPTER 5   GETTING OUT OF YOUR OWN WAY   124

CHAPTER 6   THE POWER OF INFLUENCE   138

CHAPTER 7   JUST A'LIL MORE   155

CHAPTER 8   QUICK, FAST, AND IN A HURRY   170

CHAPTER 9   "I HAVE TO USE THE BATHROOM"   178

CHAPTER 10   THE POINT OF NO RETURN   188

CHAPTER 11   SHOUT IT FROM THE MOUTAIN TOP   201

FINAL WORDS   205

ACKNOWLEDGEMENTS   208

The Roller Coaster Effect

Effect

How to Turn Your Fear into Fuel, Your Passion
into Purpose, and Enjoy the Ride of Life

INTRODUCTION

"There is no greater gift you can give or receive than to honor your calling. It is why you were born and how you become most truly alive."
– Oprah Winfrey

It was the peak of summer and what seemed to my 13-year old self to be the hottest day in St. Louis, Missouri's history. Select members of the Reedy River Missionary Baptist Church from Mauldin, South Carolina were outside in the heat taking it all in. Every year our church traveled to a chosen city to attend the National Baptist Convention. When I finally turned 13, my mother allowed me to go on the trip. Excitement came over me because I had been anxiously awaiting the day when I would be old enough to attend this convention. I knew many "firsts" would take place. I was ready to conquer them one by one. One first: this little country girl from South Carolina had *never* been on a plane. Another first: I had never met a celebrity up close and personal. Because we were in St. Louis, I thought I would bump into Nelly, one of the biggest rap stars in the early 2000's, who was from St. Louis (*Yes, I was young and naïve*). And the most important: I would ride a "ROLLER COASTER" for the first time!

The agenda allowed time for us to go to the Six Flags amusement park on one of our off days. It wouldn't be my first time at a theme park. But on previous theme park visits, every time the moment came for me to get on a ride, my stomach would do flips and my palms would sweat. The fear of getting on something so high and traveling so fast scared the life out of me. I would always find a way out of getting on a ride. If finding an excuse to go play the fun carnival skill games to win prizes didn't work, I would offer to hold everyone's book bags and backpacks since they could not be taken on the rides (*this was way before amusement parks bag bins*). But I was tired of watching all my friends get off the roller coaster with flushed faces and gushing with excitement. They discussed the weird lady standing in line in front or the fine boy in the row behind them. They also talked about the twists and the turns of the ride and the funny faces they made when the camera caught them on the final drop.

Enough was enough! I was tired of being left out! I decided *this* would be the day I would put my big

2

girl panties on and get on the ride. No longer was I going to let fear dictate my actions. This would be the day I would conquer...THE ROLLER COASTER.

We stepped off the charter bus and into the Six Flags amusement park. I was decked out in my red Tommy Hilfiger shirt, red and white flowered capris with matching red and white high-top Nike Air Force Ones, and my St. Louis Cardinals visor rocked upside down (*just as I saw the rapper Nelly wear*). When I entered the gates of the theme park, the excitement of the new challenge ahead was overwhelming.

I didn't mention my decision to my friends, just in case I didn't go through with it. I kept it to myself. By the end of the day, I was determined to mark the roller coaster off of my Bucket List. My confidence was already on a high after conquering my first airplane ride with ease. This would be a walk in the park...*I GOT THIS*, I thought to myself.

My crew walked around and scoped out what the first ride of the day would be. Then there it was. It seemed to be thousands of feet high, with twists, turns, loops, and expanses of sleek black steel that looked as though it would never end. This beast of a ride was called Batman, one of the biggest attractions at the park.

My friend yelled out, "*Let's ride this one!*"

I thought.... *Oh, SHIT!*

When they saw me following them to the line, they could not believe that I, the scaredy cat would join them this time. I was excited to take on this enormous task but the closer we got to the front of the line, the more I felt the urge to jump out of line. This was too much, too big; my expectations were too ambitious. *What was I thinking?* Maybe I needed to build my confidence up more and start with the kiddie roller coaster in Kiddy Land and maybe ride Batman *next* time. My nerves got the best of me. As we neared the line, my hands were shaking, and my heart was pounding so hard that it felt like it would jump out of my chest.

It was a week day and most of the park was deserted, except for this ride. Everyone in the park was in the line for this ride because the wait time was ridiculous. It was a good thing because the extra time before boarding helped soothe my frazzled nerves. We stood in line so long that I almost forgot that my impending death was awaiting on me at the end. But for the time being, I lived in the moment and forgot about the challenge before me. As we stood in line, we chatted about things that were going on at our schools. We argued over heart throbs, rapper Lil' Bow Wow and the boy band B2k, and prepared what we would say, should we run into Nelly.

The line was moving at a consistent pace, then suddenly, we came to a stop. We'd been waiting close to an hour. *What was happening?* It didn't seem as if the ride was stuck. It appeared to work fine. Then we heard an announcement on the loud speaker say, *"Batman will be closing today to perform maintenance. Sorry for the inconvenience."*

THANK YOU, GOD! I thought. I could have run laps around the park. I was over joyed.

I was glad I didn't have to go through with it. Whoot whoot! *I am in the clear*, I thought. Instead let's go play some games and win a few basketballs to take back to South Carolina. This was my out - I didn't fail or chicken out because it wasn't *my* fault that the ride had to be closed for maintenance. I did *try*, right?

Everyone was disappointed. This was the ride my friends were fired up to get on. But then, instead of being defeated, one friend suddenly yelled out, *"Hey, let's ride the Ninja! The line isn't even long!"*

NOOOOO! The Ninja?! What is happening? I am supposed to be in the clear. This Roller Coaster mission was supposed to be aborted!

The Ninja roller coaster seemed even more terrifying than Batman. It had more twists and turns, and repeated loops. All the relaxation in my body turned back into tension. As we stood in line for The Ninja, there were only two options - either turn around and accept failure or get on the ride and face my fears.

The choice was mine…

The Crossroads

At these pivotal moments of decision in our lives, we can walk forward into our dreams, though our stomachs may be churning, and we're filled with uncertainty, or we can turn away. A chain of emotions can get triggered when you decide to pursue your dreams or follow your passions. At first you are excited about what you can accomplish. But often, fear, anxiety, and discouragement can overtake you. Those secondary emotions are enough to make you run away and never see your dreams come to life. It can cause you to make a decision that might have permanent impact based on a fleeting feeling that is only temporary.

What causes our fear, anxiety and discouragement to come up in these pivotal moments? Brendan Burchard, the author of *The Motivation Manifesto*, explains these negative emotions arise because we connect the thoughts in our heads to pain. What if I spend this money on opening a nail salon and I don't have enough customers to stay open? And I never went to business school, who am I to think that I will succeed? Our self-talk is filled with negativity which amplifies the fear, anxiety and discouragement.

How do I know that this is true?

As a Life Coach to millennials that want to pursue their purpose, I see it in each client. Better yet I have also experienced it when launching my blog and coaching practice (*more on this in Chapter 1*). This phenomenon of wrestling with negative emotions, doubting yourself and your abilities, and this inner feeling of not knowing if you have "what it takes" to do it/succeed/pull it off, as you pursue your passion is what I refer to as *"The Roller Coaster Effect."* The Roller Coaster Effect is the overwhelming presence of fear and anxiety that can arise when you decide to act and move forward.

Think about a time when you came in contact with the person you had a huge crush on. You wanted to strike up a conversation or ask for their number but instead of doing it, you stalled, maybe stammered and fumbled the conversation. Similarly, the Roller Coaster Effect can have us talk ourselves into abandoning an idea or abandoning our passions or our dreams. It can have us feeling enthusiastic and motivated when the idea or dream first becomes clear to us, and then during the next days, weeks, or even months, we can vacillate up and down, between excitement and anxiety.

This book will develop your awareness and resilience when the Roller Coaster Effect arises in your life and in you. It will help you embrace the ride, say yes to it, and get on the ride instead of "jump ship." It will be your guide to navigating those negative emotions and breaking through self-doubt to live your dreams and pursue your passions. You will be provided with stories, exercises and reflection questions throughout the book to help you to do just that.

In Chapter 1, I share how fear almost kept me from pursuing my dream. You will come to better understand The Roller Coaster Effect and how and where it may show up in your life.

With many possible dreams and many paths available to you, how do you know what to pursue? We often pursue certain careers or hobbies because our parents want us to do, or because it will garner approval from others, or it looks glamorous on social media. When we qualify our dream, it allows us to filter the noise that may be influencing our decisions. This section will include insights to help you, clarify and qualify your dream. It will help to have a journal as a companion to this book for writing down your answers to key reflection questions that appear throughout the book. I will ask different reflection questions and personal inquiries throughout the book, and it will be very useful to have a written record of your thoughts. The journal will allow you to keep track of your responses so you can go back and re-read.

The first step to overcoming fears is to recognize them within your life. I will give insights for identifying how fear may be presenting itself in your life. I will give you steps for creating and setting your own goals on the way to fulfilling your dreams.

Then comes the fun part – metaphorically, getting ready to get in the line for the ride. You will notice how and where you may be self-sabotaging. You will learn the characteristics of the individuals you will need with you for your journey, if they are not currently present in your life, I offer suggestions on how and where you can meet them.

Social media has a lot of benefits - connecting with friends from elementary or high school, sharing tips and motivation, and staying informed of local, regional and world events. However, if you are not careful, you can be "seduced" into making jealousy-inducing comparisons and harsh self-judgement based upon the images on social media. So, I caution you of the dangers of the social disease "Comparisonitis" and how to overcome it.

Right before it is time to get on the ride, I am reminded of how we can allow fear to turn us around when we are almost at our breakthrough point. When you proceed towards your passion despite the anxiety, breakthrough the fear, and take your seat, my friend you have gotten on the ride! After reading this book you will have the blueprint to follow your dream despite the fear you experience.

Oh yeah, remember the Ninja ride I was freaking out about? I got on it and had the time of my life. You would've never known that I was scared. I rode it THREE times! Talk about a plot twist!

Are you ready to stop giving up on your dreams or thinking it is unattainable? Experience the happiness, joy, freedom, and peace that achieving your goal brings.

It's time to get on the ride and I will walk you through getting there!

CHAPTER 1

DÉJÀ VU

"Sometimes good things fall apart so better things can fall together." – Marilyn Monroe

Ten years and two degrees later…

I felt the same way as I did that day at Six Flags in St. Louis waiting to ride that roller coaster, The Ninja. The tension ran through my body; my muscles were so tight that I felt paralyzed. This time it didn't involve getting on a roller coaster but the decision to pursue my dream to be a Life Coach.

The Opportunity of a Lifetime

My educational background is in Sports Management. From the second grade on, I excelled in basketball. My sophomore year of high school, I made the Varsity team. By my junior year, I was a starter and co-captain of the team. This led to me receiving a partial scholarship to be a part of the Women's Basketball team in college. As a young basketball player, I knew that I could not play ball forever and would need to have something to fall back on. Right before I received my Master's in Sport Administration, I had the opportunity of a lifetime to meet the Vice President of Sales for the Charlotte Bobcats (now the Charlotte Hornets) a team in the NBA. He was the guest speaker in my Sport Marketing class. I'd envisioned that my adult life would revolve around basketball in some shape or form, so there was no way I would let such an opportune moment pass without me capitalizing on it. Besides sending him a handwritten *"Thank You"* letter, I also followed up with a message on the social media platform, LinkedIn, referring to an entry level Inside Sales position he mentioned during his presentation.

Prior to this moment, I made several attempts to be employed or to intern at this organization but was shot down every time. Though I was only 22 years old my dream was to climb the corporate ladder and become a top sports executive. This would be the key to open that door. And I was ready!

Days after I submitted my application, I received a call. They wanted me to come in for an interview! After months, the time had come. I was another step closer to being offered a position as an Inside Sales

Representative. My interview went great. I was offered the job, and I accepted!

It was my first day on the job. I walked into the executive suite entrance of the sports arena. It all seemed like a dream. The security guard paged my manager who came to escort me and the other new hires to the suite level where all the offices were. I peeped into a suite on an upper level of the arena and then looked down at the court. The visual took my breath away. There were thousands of seats stretching out to the left and right of me. Beholding the basketball court from rows above the game floor gave me a rush of adrenaline. In my mind, *I had made it.*

Bright-Eyed and Bushy-Tailed

That wide-angle view of the basketball court from rows above the court blew me away. And in the same way, as you approach the roller coaster ride you have anticipated getting on, you experience the same feeling as I did seeing that court. As you purchase your ticket for the amusement park, you can hear the screams from the riders' having the time of their lives. The moment becomes surreal. Your moment to get on the ride is near.

DÉJÀ VU

I remember attending a meeting at the office of a Life Coach here in Charlotte, NC. I walked in and my breath was taken away. It was all that I imagined my office to be one day. Trendy bright colored furniture, a glass conference room with a huge oak table, leather chairs, and floor to ceiling windows that gave you a beautiful view of the city. *Wow*, I thought to myself, this will one day be the type of office I will have. Though it wasn't mine in the moment, I had been exposed to what I could experience by following my dream.

I was no longer just given a glimpse of what I imagined my life to be working in the sports industry, I was now living it. The same arena that had my eyes wide open, was now the place I spent most of my days selling potential season ticket holder's seats. But the arena no longer gave me the excitement I once had. I now dreaded it. The passion wasn't one I should have been following (*we will get more into this later*) and it soon became a living hell. The job gave me validation. It represented success. When I mentioned where I worked, people were impressed. It was cool I worked in a sporting arena, frequently saw NBA stars, and watched the games for free.

However, after four months, the excitement and honeymoon phase ended. I may have felt triumphant, excited, and even major validation from others for a while, but after those four months, I felt like I was dying internally. When I was interviewing for the position, I got blinded by the prestige of being associated with the organization and I failed to ask basic questions about my job duties. I'd made assumptions that came back to haunt me. I thought that this would be a great way to get my foot in the door within a sports team and from there I could explore other departments within the organization. Well, the leadership team in the sales department wasn't down for that. If you came in as sales, you would be doing sales "forever" and nothing else.

And how did I forget to ask about the commission payment and structure? Here I was thinking that if I sold a season ticket package, I would receive the commission on my next check. That was one reason I wasn't tripping on my base pay being $17,500 annually. I was stunned when I realized that the structure was slightly different. We would not be paid until the season ticket package was paid in full. If the client went on a ten-month payment plan it could be close to a year before I cashed out (*95% of my client base were on payment plans*).

This just meant that a sistah was nearly BROKE. The position also afforded me limited room for creativity. This was something I deeply desired. However, my work routine was mundane, and morally there were tactics that didn't sit well with me. I had to lie about seat availability to push the client to purchase, when I knew that the entire section was empty. *"Yes Mr. Smith I know that you want to talk with your wife more about this. But these are the only "x" seats left in this section…"* I started counting down to when I could leave my job, even within during my first few weeks. That is when I realized - I hated my job!

The organization itself was wonderful and my co-workers were amazing. They had an active Human Resource department that kept the employees engaged; celebrating a crazy national holiday *(think National Hot Dog Day)*, sending the mascot around the office for a laugh, or having sports tournaments like kickball or dodgeball. However, when there were no events and I was tasked with doing my job; sitting in a cubicle every day selling season ticket packages in a losing year for the team, and making 100+ cold calls to people that thought the team sucked, became draining. I didn't believe in the very product I was selling, so every pitch felt like I was a phony. I also got a lot *"fluffier,"* shall we say, as I packed on the pounds sitting at a cubicle day after day, and my cheerful personality was slowly waning. It was tough. I began to hate something that I initially thought I would love for the rest of my life.

An Unexpected Sign

It was mid-day of a particular work day after ten months on the job, and I was ready to go home. I didn't want to talk to any more season ticket holder prospects that day, so I hoped no one answered the phone call. I dialed, trying to reach a gentleman who had just attended a game. I had to follow up on his experience (*i.e. trying to upsell him anything that we offered*). The phone rang and rang, and finally a middle-aged woman with a thick southern accent answered the phone. I discovered that it was his wife, so I tried to leave a message for him to call me back. But instead, she insisted on me continuing the conversation with her. I'm glad I didn't hang up because this phone call changed the trajectory of my life. What should have been a 15-minute phone call turned into a call that lasted an hour!

She was very chatty, sharing with me various details about their lives. They were raising their grandson and wanted to take him to his first professional basketball game. Thirty minutes into the conversation, I knew nearly everything about her life. Then she suddenly stopped mid-conversation and said...

Her: *"I can tell that you are covered."*

Me: *"Umm, excuse me, Ma'am?"*

Her: *"You have a family full of praying women who have you covered."*

At this point my jaw dropped —*How did she know this?* I'd made no mention of my spiritual background or how I had a praying family. I hadn't uttered a word about growing up, and every night before I went to bed, I could hear my grandmother praying. I would walk past my mother's room and see her on her knees, praying. At the end of our conversation, this woman stopped and prayed for me.

After that call, something in my spirit woke up and I knew that it was a sign of what I needed to do. I felt that God sent me confirmation that day. It was my divine sign. I could not work at this job anymore. I needed to search for another area within sports that I would enjoy. I already knew what it was: marketing. During my undergraduate years, I interned with our school's marketing department and enjoyed developing campaigns for our clients.

Divine signs can be complex to explain. We can experience them in different ways. It may come in a form of a conversation like it did for me, a lyric in a song, or a word you randomly see all the time. But what remains the same is the internal nudge or confirmation you feel. The sign is attempting to push you towards a specific action, a new direction or a next step that will be beneficial to you in some way, in either the short- or the long-term.

Ever been in the club having a good time with your friends? Then out of nowhere you get the feeling that you need to leave. There is no logic to it, but you follow it any way and go on home. Only to discover that, 30 minutes later, a brawl had broken out, people were injured, and you could have been hurt. Or have you ever had the urge to stop at a gas station you never visit, only to walk in and see an old classmate from high school – and he is looking GOOD! You exchange numbers; then start to date, and two years later get married. What if you had ignored the nudge to stop and you kept driving instead?

When you experience these nudges, don't ignore them. They could be the precursor to a life- changing moment. We may think *"something told me…"* but I'm clear that it's my intuition, and my intuition supports God's highest and best for me. The key is to learn how to trust it by heeding it.

Turn for the Worst

That pivotal conversation on the phone that day gave me what I needed to make a huge decision - was I going to continue my career in sport's sales or find a new job? A little about the program that I was a part of - the Inside Sales program teaches you the ins and outs of sales. It is a ten month to one-year development program that grooms you to take on more specific account executive positions in the organization. My year was almost up, and my manager had been breathing down my neck about which sales department I was interested in transitioning to.

The next week, I went to my manager and told him my plans. As we sat in the conference room, my

21

hands were sweaty and my heart was beating 100mph. There was no turning back now. I looked him in the eyes and told him I didn't want to do sales any longer. I wanted to look at a position in the marketing department.

The world seemed to stop. The unspoken rule in the department was sales or nothing. If you were interested in another department when you were in sales, the plot to get rid of you would begin. So yes, this was a major moment in my personal history. I had voluntarily put my head on the chopping block; but there was no way I could continue to do this job.

My manager looked at me in a state of confusion. He thought I had an interest in continuing in Group Sales where I showed many strengths. But to my surprise, after hearing me out, he seemed receptive and offered his assistance on my new job hunt. Two days later, I was called into a meeting with my manager and our director. It reminded me of being walked into the Principal's office - you know trouble is around the corner but don't know what is about to happen. Then my director said the words that I was not expecting to hear *"… Your heart just isn't in it…"* He continued to explain that if I didn't make this sales quota *(which was twice as much as our monthly sales goal)* in the next 30 days, they would have to let me go. I had written a check that my ass couldn't cash.

After our meeting, my situation was looking great. I found a possible job with an NFL team within their marketing department. My manager knew a contact at the team and would contact him to push my information forward. In the past our manager had showed us how he posted a vacant position and within an hour it had already received almost 500 job applications. So, I knew that my chances for an interview would increase if I had a direct connection in the organization. Two weeks before my 30-day timeframe my manager had a conversation with one of their managers. He told me that he'd put in a good word for me, and it went well. He said that they should be contacting me soon regarding an interview. A day went by, a week went by, two weeks passed and still nothing. Now the NFL dude wasn't responding to me nor my manager's follow-up emails. My bright hopes turned dark again. I thought, maybe I got it all wrong. Maybe I was supposed to stay. I had noting lined up and my 30-day timeframe is coming down to the wire. Through all the doubt and uncertainty, all I could hear was the lady's voice from that phone call whispering in my ear "*You are covered...*" **Thirty days later... I was fired.**

On my last day, instead of being sad, I expressed joy to my co-workers. I was about to escape the hell hole I felt I was in. I was glad to be leaving this place. Still, though I was leaving, on inside I felt lost and didn't know how I would survive financially. I barely had $100 in my checking account. I thought, I could always move back to South Carolina with my family, but that had *"FAIL-URE"* written all over it. I was the #GirlBoss that everyone was so proud of and moving back home meant that I had failed them and also let myself down.

During my period of unemployment, I avoided everyone. Not once during this period did, I go to South Carolina to visit my family. My friends would invite me out to parties or dinners and I would find a way to get out of it. And if I did say yes, I would then call them last minute and tell them that something came up and I couldn't make it. I didn't want to face the fact that I was fired. I knew that everyone would have a million questions about what happened, questions I didn't want to answer.

For the next three months, I locked myself away in my apartment, only leaving periodically to go to church. I found solace there. I couldn't wait until Sunday – it was the only day I felt hope that my situation might change for the better. One Sunday, I didn't intentionally go to church but I ended up there on accident. My mentor, Ms. Martha Gamble Hall, just had surgery and could not drive and asked me if I could take her to church. As I sat in service feeling defeated by my situation, I felt that the Pastor was speaking directly to me. He preached a series about Daniel, who refused to submit to false gods and was thrown into the lion's den and later promoted as a top official in Babylon. He served and interpreted the dreams of King Nebuchadnezzar. King Nebuchadnezzar had a bazaar dream that involved a tree being stripped down to its roots and him having a mind of an animal for seven years. Daniel interpreted the dream as the king transforming from being a powerful ruler to being driven away from people and living like an animal. King Nebuchadnezzar would return to his rule once he recognized that God held the power over the kingdom. After a year passed, all that Daniel predicted would happen, did.

King Nebuchadnezzar came to this point after

seven years in the wilderness. *"At the end of that time I, Nebuchadnezzar looked up toward heaven. My mind became clear again…My honor and glory were returned to me when my mind became clear again. The glory of my kingdom was given back to me. My advisers and nobles came to me. And I was put back on my throne. I became even greater than I had been before."* (Daniel 4:34-36).

I felt like that was me. I had accomplished much at this point but I felt like it had all been stripped away. It was time for me to *"look towards heaven"* and get connected with God. I prayed, spent time reading my Bible, and attending Bible Study. My lifestyle even changed. I no longer felt the urge to get drunk all the time. I decided to end a three-year toxic sexual relationship and became celibate. This evolution took me almost five months. After those five months, for the first time since being fired, I felt I could make it. I felt that I'd be able to get through this tough time.

For three long months, I searched high and low, and shook my contacts for a position in the sports world. After several interviews, I finally landed a job in a very different industry, the banking industry within mortgage, far from a position related to sports. It wasn't ideal by any means, but it paid the bills.

A Dream Realized

In banking, I worked with an older generation. Many of them talked about chasing their dreams but instead, not many of them ever did. *I didn't want that to be my story.* Meanwhile, I realized that the sports industry wasn't where my passion was, but I felt there had to be a greater calling on my life than being in sales.

Meanwhile, I became an avid reader. I like how I felt after reading – like I could accomplish anything. I felt motivated, unstoppable, and invincible. I knew I wanted other people to feel the same way. One day I might write a book, I thought. Then I'd laughed hysterically in my head. Me?? The same person in remedial reading and writing as a kid and still a terrible speller to this day. Clearly, I wasn't a writer. But if I wanted to birth a book, I had better start writing.

I was motivated to write out advice I recently gave a friend. He was talking about how he hated his job and was looking for a new one. After he left my house, I thought *"Man, he is a runaway employee."* That was the title of my first article. After I read it, I sent it to my

27

brother Julius, my cousin Charmaine, and my sorority sister Cherrelle. They all read it and responded the same thought.

You need to start a blog!

Start a blog? Yeah, right!

I thought of every reason I couldn't do it. *Not enough time. That's an area I know little about. My writing isn't good enough. My grammar SUCKS!* Every suggestion from others to start a blog was followed by a litany of internal excuses of why I couldn't or why it wouldn't work. For months I ran from this idea. Relating this back to the amusement park, it reminded me of how we can try to hide in Kiddy Land to avoid getting on the rollercoaster.

What is Kiddy Land? Kiddy Land can represent many things in our lives: the mediocre situations or the crumbs we settle for in our lives; avoiding our greatness or withholding the gifts and talents we know should be used in the world. Instead we watch from afar, wishing we could ride with the big, thrilling ride with the "*big kids.*" But what we should realize is that *WE CAN!* I'm inviting you to get off the kiddy land merry go round, and let's get you on that roller coaster!

28

I had done this numerous of times at the amusement park – dodging the rollercoaster and finding ways to waste away the time in Kiddy Land. I seemed to have an internal tug-of -war going on. I wanted it – I did. But I was also so scared that I wouldn't succeed at it. There was an internal tug of war - passion on one side and fear tugging away on the other. It reminded me of standing and looking up at the roller coaster, excited for what I would experience on it. But then the grip of fear preventing me from getting on it. But I was tired of this internal battle, and I was also tired of running from this new opportunity that kept re-presenting itself to me.

One day I was walking to my cubicle at my new mortgage job. A lady displayed her 30 years of service certificate on her desk. I sat thinking to myself, how could someone do this for 30 years?! I haven't been there for even four months and I was already going crazy from boredom and redundancy. But if I didn't make a change, that might be me.

In that moment, the realization hit me: *I was in charge of what my life looks like and I am the person best-equipped to change its direction.* It clicked for me in that moment. I would not waste my life away going from job to job, doing something that made me miserable. It was time for me to go for it! And starting the blog would be the first step in bringing my dream to life.

Have you noticed? There will always seem to be reasons you shouldn't or can't pursue your dream. And those negative thought and self-doubting inner conversations are what we usually allow to dictate our time. If you do not rewire your thinking, there will always seem to be a barricade or insurmountable obstacles to not go after it. But you have the power to break through those initial thoughts of doubt and feelings of discouragement.

Here is an exercise to help you re-wire how your brain thinks, if self-defeating thoughts keep arising at moments or points when you have an opportunity for growth or expansion. Instead of reacting with low-level thoughts about inadequacy, consider another option that would generate new possibilities instead of defeat or a dead end? In other words, look for a way to counter the self-defeating thought that opens up new possibilities.

Initial thought: *"I could never start an online clothing boutique. I have student loans and I don't have the money for it."*

Response: *"What if I researched how much it would cost, then look at the various ways to raise capital or purchase the merchandise?"*

Initial thought: *"I don't have the time to go back to school to finish my degree."*

Response: *"What if I found a program that had night classes and tailored for working professionals?"*

Initial thought: *"I can't apply for that job, I don't have the experience."*

Response: *"What if I found a way to create experience by speaking with my manager and asking for additional roles in my current position?"*

It reminds me of a line from a poem written by Erin Hanson. *"What if I fall? Oh. But, my darling, what if you fly."*

So, I acted on the response question and started my research. Day and night, I researched the elements that needed to be included for this blog. I decided on a name: *The Fear Hurdler.* A to-do list was created with a launch date a month away. However, the date came and went: *still no blog*. Four months passed and I felt as though I was still not ready. I was still playing self-defeating "tapes" in my head. *What would people say about my blog? I'm not really a writer. What if no one visits the site? What happens if I run out of things to say?* The worries ran so rampant in my head that I became dizzy. Anxiety was high. But it wasn't too late. There was still time to delete the website and no one would ever know it ever existed.

There it was again…*The Roller Coaster Effect*. The fear of *"getting on the ride"* was overwhelming me. This time the stakes were bigger. I could let fear win, close my laptop and neglect my dreams, or I could launch my new blog, *The Fear Hurdler*, thus making it available to the world!

What is The Roller Coaster Effect?

When you first saw the title *"The Roller Coaster Effect,"* you might have thought I was going to be talking about the twists and turns that life brings, which can be equated to the twists and turns you experience once you get on a rollercoaster. Yes, this is true, however, the Roller Coaster Effect is what can occur *before* you even get on the ride. The Roller Coaster Effect is the overwhelming presence of doubt, worry and fear that can grip us and encourages us to abandon our dreams, and have second (and third) thoughts, even before you get on the ride. The Roller Coast Effect can kick in while you're inching yourself closer and closer to the front of the line. When fear presents itself, you will feel an urge to run out of the line. *But what are you going back to?* Perhaps a mediocre un-fulfilling life in which you are merely existing and not living, or a job that pays the bill *(and well)* - *but it doesn't make your heart sing.*

Living is about waking up every day feeling excited of what's to come, a peace of mind, and experiencing internally a joy indescribable Best-selling author and life coach Barbara Sher once said *"As soon as you start to pursue a dream, your life wakes up and everything has meaning."* That's a result of getting on the ride. You may be scared, and that's ok. You can still keep putting one foot in front of the other, moving closer with each step, towards the *"new thing,"* the new experience or the opportunity to stretch you or enable you to offer your gifts, talents and skills to the world. But once you get on the ride, and strap in, your life can change - forever.

I decided to *"get on the ride"* and launch my blog

five months after the initial launch date. Then two years later, I started my coaching practice, also entitled *"The Fear Hurdler."* Let me share with you the crazy story of how I came up with the name.

When I was at the point of possibly deleting the site, I still didn't have a name for it. One night I prayed *"God if this is what you want me to do, you will give me a name. If not, I'm going back to forgetting that this blog idea ever happened."* As I lay down to sleep that same night, a thought slammed into my head - The Fear Hurdler: Overcoming obstacles to reach your dreams. That's it! That is what it will be called! I jumped up and grabbed my iPhone to record the name. Guess that was God's way of telling me that there was no turning back!

The decision to pursue my dream allowed me to live a life filled with satisfaction. Before I only found excitement when anticipating trips or events. Now, with my blog and coaching practice, every morning I woke up knowing I can pour motivation, inspiration and change into someone's life. Now I can't wait to start the day. But it started with me not just having jobs that looked good on paper, but living a fulfilled life, *"getting on the ride."*

DÉJÀ VU

You will always have a choice. Will you run out of line or get on the ride? How about leave a life of complaining, wishing, and hoping to do what you really want to do in life? Or maybe it is the choice to finally confront your fear or to live out your dream? The decision is up to you.

CHAPTER 2

PREPARE FOR THE JOURNEY

"You turn on my fire, baby and you burned me up within your flame. Took me a little higher, made me live again..." — Rick James

"I know I can, be what I wanna be. If I work hard at it, I'll be where I wanna be." — Nas

Imagine this. You are about to climb a tall mountain which stands over 10,000 feet in height. As you lift your head in amazement, you realize this will be a daunting journey - a daunting journey because of the height, the vertical distance, the stamina required and the possibilities of challenges, crevasses, and difficulties along the way. However, once you make it to the top, step by step, you will experience a view that will take your breath away.

Just like the hike up the mountain, reaching fulfillment is a journey. It's about the process, each step along the way, and the journey — not just the final destination. You may face hardships and discouragement that make you feel like giving up, but when you reach the top, the feeling of fulfillment and victory can actually change your entire perspective and make every step worth it. I've found that this *"view from the mountain top"* can literally change both you and your life. You probably are curious about how this can happen. Well, first let's start with getting a better understanding of what fulfillment is.

Get off the Merry Go Round

Fulfillment is an inner experience that eludes most people. It seems to be a far-fetched concept discussed on Oprah Winfrey's *Super* Soul Sunday that we always seem to chase. Fulfillment is defined as satisfaction that results from developing one's abilities or character, or the achievement of something desired, promised, or predicted. Fulfillment is the feeling within your soul when you are immersed in an experience that resonates with your being. Fulfillment is experienced when you are on the path to your dreams and following your passion. If you are a Millennial like me, we tend to follow occupations or jobs based on what will make us money, and not our interest in the organization. We'll almost settle for anything that helps us to pay back the outrageous student loans we've accumulated. Gallup recently conducted a study that 71% of Millennials have no emotional commitment to their organization or its goals.

Unfortunately, we spend an average of over 40 hours a week there. Why not utilize that time to do something we can connect to? The *"amusement park"* of life is filled with many attractions, and even distractions, and so many rides that the possibilities can seem overwhelming at first. Then you see it. The biggest and most thrilling ride you have ever laid your eyes on. Though it is everything you have ever desired and more, you ask yourself, *"How could I get on something this big, this exciting?*

You watched YouTube videos all week to learn about this ride and to prepare to ride it. But then, when it's right there in front of you, fear takes over. You get cold feet. This is when the Roller Coaster Effect kicks in: the power of fear makes you hesitate to get on the ride. So, you punk out and go to kiddy land instead. You opt to bypass fulfillment. You pursue a career for a paycheck. You play it safe. You play small. How often has this happened in our lives in various forms and in various ways?

Why Does Passion Matter?

I know you probably hear a lot today about passion. But what is it and how can it fuel you to go after your dream?

Passion is an inner fuel that ignites a burning desire, an intense enthusiasm, within. It can move you to work harder, and it can activate a deeper inner reservoir that gives you the ability to work through obstacles when most people would otherwise quit. The beauty about discovering your passion is that it can give you important clues about your personal mission - the reason you exist.

When I think of passion, it reminds me of a story from my childhood. As a young girl, my family did not have central air and heat. This meant that during the summer our house was filled with electric fans, and then when winter hit, the kerosene heater was pulled out and plugged in. For all the young, non-country folks, a kerosene heater is a cylinder heater that stands about 3 ½ ft. tall. At the base is a knob and a window door right above it. The knob controls the wick that is lit by a match. At the top of the heater crown were holes that allowed the heat to escape.

I got excited when I was finally old enough to light the wick all by myself. Really, I don't know why I was so happy. There was something about being able to light the wick that would then warm the house that made me feel as if I was saving the world, or at least my family, from the cold. I took my little hand and turned the wick knob as if my life depended on it. After watching my grandmother do this what seemed like ten million times, I thought I had it down pat. I crouched down to light it up. After what seemed like 25 tries, I would finally get the match to strike. Man, oh man, my eyes lit up when I saw the blaze run ignite the wick. Yep, in my mind, I had just saved the world – or least my household.

But before I could parade around the house with my chest poked out, believing I rescued everyone from freezing to death, the flame burned for three seconds and then disappeared. I tried it again, and did just what I was told. After several tries, I couldn't figure out why it wasn't working. Each time, the flame would die out after a few seconds. I couldn't understand why. I followed the directions I was given to the tee. Finally, after being unable to figure this mystery out by myself and getting highly frustrated, I told my Grandma that something must be wrong with her heater. She asked me if there was any gas in it.

Gas? I had to check that? Nobody mentioned gas!

I looked at the gauge only to see the red needle was past the E! The solution was simple – the wick wouldn't stay lit because it didn't have gas – the necessary fuel. Passion is the fuel.

Though you may be educated, it isn't enough to keep the heater going. Without the fuel, you will continue to be frustrated. You can use match, after match. You can go through the proper motions, again and again, but the flame won't be sustained. Passion is your "*sustaining fuel.*"

Make sense why some things don't seem to work out, huh? Could it be that passion is missing?

How do you know what you are passionate about? You may be thinking that you don't get that excitement eager feeling about anything. To discover your passion, here are two guidelines to assist you along the way.

1. The answer is right there

41

Your passion could be right in front of you; however, you may be missing out or missing it because you are refusing to notice it, not able to notice it, or you won't give it a chance. You know the moment when you give a thought a HARD NO; by rejecting the possibility your perspective can become limited causing you to miss out. Picture this, your future husband/wife may be package as the friend you have put in the "friend zone" (when a friend has a crush but you are less than interested).

2. Passion can be found amongst the details

We must take a moment to look more closely at the details of our lives, this is where our talents can be found. Talents are often the vehicle for the expression of our passions. We will then notice talents that provide us insight to our passion. I will share how my talent to connect with strangers was hiding behind the fact that I had athletic abilities.

Creating a path for your future can be intimidating and even overwhelming; but as we walk through these points your vision will become clearer on what your passion involves. As ideas pop into your head reading this portion, write them down as you go. Be prepared to experience an ah-ha moment. You know, the moment when things all make sense! Let's get into it.

The Answer is Right There

I'm what society calls a hopeless romantic. I love to hear or see a good love story. My favorite type to hear is when a couple starts off as great friends only to discover that the guy was madly in love with the girl the entire time. She didn't view him in the same manner. *"I would never date him; he is just my friend,"* she thinks to herself. Then it happens. It's not as if a brick hit her upside the head. But something *does* happen. In an illuminating moment, she notices him in a new way. She sees him in a new light and notices what she hasn't noticed before. And in that instant, everything changes. She suddenly becomes open to having a relationship with her *"best friend."* She was searching high and low for a healthy love relationship, and didn't realize that *"her love"* was right there, "under her nose" and right in front of her the entire time.

What in your life are you adamantly or even stubbornly, saying NO to? There is a chance you are missing out on your passion. It could be right under your nose. How do you give it a chance?

The short answer is - stop disqualifying yourself, consider possibilities instead, and learn how to reframe

43

your mindset.

Instead of thinking…

"Hmmm, I don't know the right people…"

"I don't have the money…"

"I'm not smart enough to pursue that…"

"No one in my family has ever done it…"

Try re-framing your thoughts and your mindset instead.

To combat these defeating thoughts, work at re-framing your mindset about it. Reframing replaces negative thoughts with positive ones and has you see things differently. This allows you to view your situation in another perspective. Those thoughts, inside of a new frame, can transform your perception, your perspective, and what previously were objections or obstacles. A new question can create a new frame: *"What if I was to consider it? What if it were the springboard to new opportunities?"* And the questions that previously arose when you were aligned with a *"No way,"* are now reframed to be aligned with questions that hold new possibilities instead.

"Where can I meet the right people?"

"If I start saving now, I will have the money that I need…"

"I could take a class to learn more about this…"

"What if I do it and others in my family are inspired and decide to follow in my footsteps?"

And instead of fixating on your limitations or *"catastrophizing"* and imagining the worst outcomes, turn it inside out and *consider the possibilities*! Limitation-focused thinking will prevent you only from opening your mind and giving yourself the space to develop your passion to your fullest potential. Your answer is there, now is the time to alter your perspective to see it clearly.

Passion is in the Details

Where is Waldo? Seriously, where is that little sucker? He is always hiding out somewhere. If you don't know who Waldo is, it was a popular book in the 1990's/2000's. The pages were filled with drawings crammed with hundreds of people in the pictures and you would have to find the guy named Waldo amid it. If you looked at the pictures too quickly or not enough, nine times out of 10, you would miss Waldo. It wasn't until you paid close attention to the details you would locate him in the crowd. And to throw you off, the artist includes several others in the picture that could be mistaken for Waldo, unless you looked closely.

Your passion may not be noticeable at first; it may not be obvious or screaming at you as you view your life. Looking at the bigger picture it may not seem to be there. However, after greater attention to the details and focusing in, you will find it has been there *all along.* Just like Waldo; it is there, somewhere, but we must pay close attention for him to be found.

Here are two tips to assist you in looking closely in your life and uncovering your passion.

Detail #1 - Discover your true T

What are your talents? You may be thinking there is no way your talents can be linked to your passion or that you possess none. It's time to *look closer.*

For me, I always thought my ability to play basketball was my only ticket to success. From the age of seven, my identity became based upon my athletic ability.

After winning various MVP awards and All-Star appearances in high school, the entire city came to know me as *"The Girl That Can Play Ball."* It carried me all the way to college. So, my obvious choice was to become a women's college basketball player but I missed out on discovering so much more. There were so many other talents I had overlooked or taken for granted.

When I focused my lens, I could immediately connected with people. If we met, you would probably leave the conversation with the feeling that we had known each other for years. For example, one day I was sitting outside a restaurant on a bench waiting for my who-never-seem-to-be-on-time friends to arrive, I started a conversation with a lady sitting beside me. In that short span of 15 minutes, I discovered her occupation, childhood memories, and why her youngest daughter left interior design and became a hairstylist. My late-as-hell friends arrived just as me and my *"new best friend"* were saying our goodbyes.

"Where do you know her from?" They asked. *"Oh, we just met a few minutes ago,"* I replied. They all gave me a look of suspicion as though I was lying. *"How in the hell do you get people to open up to you so fast like that? I can barely*

get people to say hello to me!" one friend voiced. Yes, this was one ability showing up!

You may not know where to start in the *"natural talents and abilities"* discovery process. Here are three questions to ask yourself to help you gain clarity. Ask yourself:

1. *What do people often ask me how to do?*

_____

_____

_____

_____

2. *What types of things do people seek my advice or feedback on?*

_____

_____

_____

_____

_____

3. *What is it that people study or train for to do that seems to come naturally for me?*

_____

_____

_____

_____

_____

Now, take a moment and write down your answers to these three questions in the lines provided above.

Detail #2 - What do you like?

Duh, if you will spend your time doing something, you should at least like to do it. That would be common sense. *What do you enjoy?* I mean *really* enjoy? A great indicator is if no one paid you a dollar to do it, would you still be excited and eager to engage and complete the task?

What is it you'd be doing? What are you doing when time seems to fly?

_____

_____

_____

_____

_____

What are you doing when you're so immersed that you lose track of time?

_____

_____

_____

_____

_____

What does this look like?

_____

_____

_____

_____

_____

Think about your job. We all have that Negative Nancy in the office. When the manager asks her to complete a new task her response is always, "*that's not in my job description.*" She opts out of doing it. You don't fuss and complain when given additional task because you enjoy what you do.

I had been blogging for over a year before I made any money from my website. But I enjoyed doing it. I was excited to hit "*publish*" on a new article, whether I made any money or not. I still love that I get to sit down and write a story with tips and insight that can help someone accomplish a dream they didn't think is possible. It still amazes me when I receive emails or messages on social media about how a blog post has impacted someone's life.

Writing has also become therapeutic and form of self-care. Many stories that I have shared, I have never talked with anyone about. So, when I am writing it allows me to process it and ask questions I would otherwise ignore or avoid. I was excited to complete the task with or without a check attached to it.

There is a progression to arrive to your purpose. Your passion is the gateway which gives you a burning desire for more *(when I felt the need inspire others)*. It drives you to become aware of your dream; which is the vision of what you would like to accomplish *(when I saw myself blogging and coaching)*. As you begin to have action towards your dream then you gain insight of your purpose; your personal mission in life, also referred to as your WHY.

What is Your WHY?

I grew up in a single parent home with my two brothers. We weren't ballin' financially but we had just enough to get by. My mother sacrificed so much to meet our needs by working extra shifts or pitching pennies...*literally*. As a kid I would hate when she would fill up a plastic bag of coins to give me for my lunch money. You could hear me jingling down the school hallways before you ever saw me. It wasn't until I was around 13-year-old that I peeked into her bedroom one night only to see her scraping together change so I could purchase lunch at school the next day. It wasn't because she wanted to give me all those coins; it was all she had.

So, what has driven me to excel in school and now in my career? I desire to be in a financial situation that enables me to give my mom any and everything that she desires. When I feel like quitting, I think about that house I want to buy her, and I go back to work. But that isn't my only Why. When I share my story (being fired from my sports team sales job from Chapter 1), others began to ask me about God. How did I develop a relationship with God? I was often asked. They saw God working in my life and wanted to experience something

52

similar. I didn't realize that by pursuing my dream I would be drawing people closer to God or creating a curiosity to know him better. It gave my purpose a greater meaning, and a boost, and compelled me to continue to fulfill my passion no matter how much fear attempted to turn me away. I didn't realize how much I talked about my faith in my blog posts and videos on Instagram. Well, I didn't realize this until I had a coaching call with a client and my client posed a question. *"how were you able to develop a relationship with God?"* I wasn't sure how to answer the question at first, and just responded with some of my practices: prayer, reading and studying the Bible, and surrounding myself with others with the same faith. A couple days later on a different coaching call, the same question was brought up. I noticed how people were asking me in various ways the same question. How can I have a relationship with God? I was surprised. I am no preacher or minister and didn't feel like I was worthy enough to be guiding others to God. I was looking at my imperfections and my shortcomings, but God was using those things; my battles with ego, my quest to find my purpose in life, even me lying about getting fired - all to bring people closer to Him. It was almost like I had started a *"Millennials trying to live for Christ"* ministry without knowing it.

53

After re-considering your No's and a new perspective to your talents, take a moment and write down your passions. For example, mine reads: to educate and inspire others to fear less living so that they can pursue their passions and follow their God-given purpose. Now, it's your turn!

_____

_____

_____

_____

Reflect on this for a moment. *What drives your desire to reach your dreams?* Answer these questions to assist you in developing your why:

1. What gives you a burning desire for more in life?

_____

_____

_____

_____

2. In what ways could you use your strengths to add value to the world?

_____

_____

_____

_____

_____

3. Have you ever noticed a force seeming to nudge you along to continue to make certain choices and pursue your dreams? If so, explain that experience, when you've noticed it, and how it feels when it's happened.

_____

_____

_____

_____

_____

      Writing out the answers to these questions will help you to realize your why. Once you complete the exercise, write your why out where you can see it. I wanted to do something that I felt mattered in the world, and I would impact people and allow them to experience the new-found happiness that confronting my fears allowed me to experience. The benefits of living from this place of happiness are many: the freedom allows me to

55

be authentic and do what I want to do versus fitting into someone else's mold. When I was in denial, it seemed as though every conversation I had was related to assisting *others* with *their* dreams. For example, I could be in a night club and meet a guy, and before I know it, the guy would be pouring his heart out to me about his aspirations, fears and what he really wanted to do in life.

Besides being a driving force, your Why also keeps you focused. In a day, there are several decisions you'll make, and hundreds of choices. But if they aren't consistent with your Why, you can make decisions that are a distraction, or take you off-path from fulfilling your passion instead of closer to it, step by step. Having your Why written down helps you maintain clarity, assess in the moments you are deciding, and make the right and aligned decisions.

Now that you understand what drives you, it is now time to shed the imposed desires that others have for your life. If you fail to; just like at an amusement park, you will leave the park with regret because you never got on the rides you wanted to get on.

Is That You?

Life can seem like Halloween - we put on so many masks that we can forget what our real face looks like. You wear a mask for so long, you can forget who you are beneath it, or that you're even wearing a mask. The mask can be derived from the expectations that other people have of us, a way of behaving is conditioned, that we learned or acquired as a survival or protective mechanism, because it represents what is socially more accepted or validated or is considered more accomplished. With every expectation, to please others, to fit in, or because we don't want to disappoint other people, we put a new mask on or unknowingly adhere our current one to our faces even more tightly. When we try to fit into the norm of others, it can cause us to relinquish our commitment to our passion and even move away from being our authentic self.

Behind our masks can be conditioned norms and thoughts such as:

"I have to get married, have kids, and move into a house in this zip code."

"If I don't work at this company, I won't have social status in this

city"

I can't go natural with my hair - what will they think at church?

"I can't start a homemade jewelry business because self-employment is not an acceptable occupation by my parents."

"I can't drive a used car; it must be brand new. People will think that I am broke!"

We don't realize that putting on airs to be accepted or esteemed, ultimately results in feeling empty. Why? Because our motive is arising from trying to fulfill someone *else's* expectations for us or of us. We lose our true selves. We look up and realize that our identity is superficial, has no deep roots, and is based upon externally imposed "requirements" we've allowed to be imposed on us by others. Well, it is time to meet yourself again and reintroduce you to...YOU!

I know this story all too well. One day I woke up and didn't recognize myself. I wore not one but several masks: I was wearing the mask of wanting to fit in; the mask of acting a particular way at work because I was the only Black woman in the office, the mask of adjusting my taste in men so my friends would except the guy I was dating, and the mask of working at a certain place to fit other's standards of success, just to name a few. These things led me to a string of unnecessary heartbreaks.

During this time, all of my friends were in relationships. They were boo'd up. I didn't want to be the odd person out. I repeatedly sent the 2:00am after-the-club-let-out text message to a guy that had no serious interest in me. This meant me going above and beyond trying to get a guy to *"change"* his mind about me and even trying to talk him into wanting to be with me. Hell, I didn't want to be the only one without a "boo!" I'm not saying that everyone wants or needs to be in a committed relationship. But that was what I thought I had to have. I also was trying to land a job so I could *"look"* fabulous and stunt on social media. You know, posting pictures as if I was living my best life (*even if I wasn't*); courtside at the game (*oww*), yes, I met Nelly (*FINALLY! Check me out!*), and I took a picture of my meal at an upscale restaurant (*nom nom nom*). I was wearing so many layers of masks that I woke up one day not knowing or recognizing the person I was looking at in the mirror. I didn't recognize myself anymore, and I certainly didn't like who the person had become who was staring back at me.

I'd lost myself. I wanted to-find the real Jasmine again, the person I was before I layered on the masks, trying to fit in with the rest of the world.

Now what does this have to do with the Roller Coaster Effect *and pursuing your dreams?* Glad you asked. If you don't know who you are, then you are highly susceptible to someone telling you who you are. In life we can experience the same feeling from mask-wearing - there is something missing. You have fulfilled everyone else's dream but not your own. *So, who are you, really? "Be yourself--not your idea of what you think somebody else's idea of yourself should be."* --Henry David Thoreau. When you know who you are; you can stand firm when those around you attempt to impose their ideas of what you should do.

It is About You, Not Them

Those around us can have good intentions but apply pressure to the point we feel we will break. Just imagine being a *twentysomething, educated, cute, accomplished woman* but single. Now imagine this woman walking into a family get-together. My oh my, the comments you can get!

"When are you going to bring a man home?"

"Why aren't you married yet?"

"What's wrong with you?"

The interrogation begins. Your family wants you to be in a loving relationship, but you may not be interested in dating. Because of all this pressure you feel the need for a boo. You know how it goes. The ex-boo sends a *"Hey, stranger"* message on Facebook. Of course, they don't have your number. You either blocked them or changed it after the breakup *(which should be a red flag to run the other way).* This isn't simply a casual, *"I want to see how you are"* message, but a loaded "Hey, Stranger" in as *"I want my baby back so let me back into your life"* message.

Your initial reaction is *"Hell to the nah!"* However, the pressure begins to play devil's advocate. There's been a vacancy for a boo for some time now. And your mother hasn't shut up about wanting grandkids. At the last family gathering, she prayed that you would find a mate ….and soon. Have there been times where the pressure from others compels you to do certain things? Or other's comments start to really get to you? Instead of following your own truth, and being true to self, the negative pressure from others moves you to do something that is in the opposite direction of your own heart's desire.

And you react.

The thoughts and opinions of others can weigh heavily on us and can affect us greatly – especially those who have known us a long time or are related to us. It's what you desire in your heart of hearts over what others want for you. Remember, the goals others (especially parents) imposes on us may reflect their own unfulfilled dreams or unexpressed passions. It's time to give yourself a reality check: Ask yourself two questions. *How have other's expectation hindered me from living a life I desire? Are my goals truly my goals, and do they goals serve my highest interest?* If it is for your higher purpose and higher interest, then you are on the right track. If you ask yourself these questions and it's to appease someone else, or a version of someone else's goals for you, then do not pass go, do not collect $200 *(Did you catch the Monopoly game reference?)*.

If you strip away the expectations of others,

what remains? What do you truly want? We call this your dream. We will take a moment to get clear on what your dream is.

What Do I Want?

A barrier that prevents us from pursuing our dream results from a lack of clarity. We have no sense of what we desire, in our heart of hearts. If a magic genie appeared and granted you any three wishes, related to your dreams, what would they be? Write these below:

1. _____
   _____
   _____
   _____

2. _____
   _____
   _____
   _____

3. _____
   _____
   _____
   _____

Don't get caught up on *how* it will happen. We will get to that shortly. The focus of this question is to first help you GET CLEAR. But knowing *what* you want, with clarity, allows you to "*see it*," even feel it, and then create an attainable plan to get there. It is amazing how the Universe works on your behalf the moment you get clear on what you want. The Universe is waiting for each of us – via our thoughts and words, to clearly tell it what we want. Once we do then it, it becomes responsive and is "*wired*" to deliver on our dominant thoughts. The novel, *The Alchemist* says "*And when you want something, all the Universe conspires in helping you to achieve it.*" The Bible also talks about stating your desires in Matthew 7:7: "*Ask and it will be given to you; seek and you will find; knock and the door will be opened to you.*" The key is that you must first know what you want so you can then ask for it.

I Believe I Can Fly…I Think?

At church one day we had a guest speaker, Dr. Dennis Kimbro, the author of *Think and Grow Rich: A Black Choice*. He told a story about an eagle that has stuck with me to this day. It was that impactful. I will share some of it with you. I will change the pronoun to she in the story.

There was once an eagle who was confused about who she was. She didn't realize that she was born into a brood of chickens. She noticed that she was not like the other chickens. Though they did not outright make her feel awkward, she didn't feel completely "*at home*" either. One day she flapped her wings; but the other chickens asked, *"What are you doing? You know us chickens don't fly."* She thought to herself *"If I am not supposed to fly, why do I have a desire to spread my wings and fly?"* Feeling as though she was trapped, she knew that something wasn't right but didn't know what it was. So, she stopped flapping her wings.

One day while she was playing with the other chickens, she looked overhead in amazement at someone that looked just like her. She rushed to her mother and questioned her about where she came from. Her mother replied, *"I went to the hen house one day and you were there. I knew you were not a chicken, but I wasn't going to love you any less. You are an eagle. It is time for you to fly and leave the chicken coop. The day is here that I knew would come when you would want to spread your wings and fly."*

The eagle had these huge beautiful wings and she was designed for flight, but it wasn't until she recognized the truth of who she was and shed her false identity she spread her wings to take flight. She had everything that she needed to fly and to soar; *she was equipped. But first, she had to leave her old beliefs and her false self-concept behind.*

Do you know and believe that you can make your dreams come true? Do you know and believe that what you desire can someday be your reality?

We create these fiction stories inside our heads based upon our perceived inadequacies or imposed, false identities. For every shortcoming, we create a new inner conversation that supports our inadequacies. *What is your "shortcoming" story? What false beliefs are in the way? What justifications are you using?* Write your response to these questions here:

_____

_____

_____

_____

_____

_____

_____

_____

_____

_____

_____

_____

_____

For example, I told myself there was no way I could be a writer. I didn't know the proper rules of grammar, and spell check was still correcting me on *their and there*. So, you want to be a writer: *Girl, bye.* The moment we decide to achieve more in life, negative emotions and thoughts can pop up to challenge our new resolve. These "*old*" emotions and thoughts are actually "*rising to the top*" because they contradict our new resolve. You'd rather they rise up so you can "*let them out*" and release them instead of continuing to hold them inside of yourself. Don't let these "*old*" emotions and thoughts cause you to stay inside of a box or a bubble and never move forward in your personal mission. If this little naysaying voice is given too much "*air time*," it can take you over. You can get paralyzed. This technique I will share will assist you with taking control of the negative conversation and transforming it through visualization.

One technique I use is *replacing doubt with hope by using visualization.* Visualize, I mean really see yourself where you want to be, in full color, as if you were there and doing it, right now. Take a few minutes right now to do this. Engage all of your senses. Visualize and imagine it down to the sounds, colors, smells, tastes, how you feel, how you are walking, talking, dressing, who is around you, what is going on? Pull no punches. When I say *believe BIG, I mean let it rip, with no holds barred.* Place no limitations on the possibilities.

Then I invite you to turn your visualization into a description. And here's the key: write it in the *present* tense, as if it was so, *right now.* Remember, present tense…. (Hint: use no *–ing* endings on words, or *–ed* ending on words; use only present tense words.)

When you do your visualization, what do you "see" as a possibility? Write it here:

_____

_____

_____

_____

_____

_____
_____
_____
_____
_____
_____
_____
_____
_____
_____
_____
_____
_____
_____

How was that exercise for you?

After completing this exercise for myself, working my current full-time job was not included in my visualization. I described at length the different programs, speaking engagements, coaching, and books that I would write and inspire others through. I would also continue to teach as an adjunct professor because it brought me joy to impact college students. It led me to believe big and I made the declaration I would quit my full-time position. I didn't worry about how financially it would happen, but I made the declaration and began to believe that it could happen. It was possible for me.

"And when you want something, all the Universe conspires in helping you to achieve it." That is exactly what began to happen. The following Monday I attended a training for Life Coaches. The last portion of the training was a laser coaching session. This session is only 15 to 20 minutes long and you can work through one goal or situation, real time, with a Life Coach. There were signs all around the room showing all the Life Coaches with whom you could meet, from parenting, to fitness, business, and career. As we were dismissed to sit with the topic or area we desired to talk about, the coaching slots seemed to fill up. But to my surprise, I looked to my right and guess who was with no one at his station? Remember the coach's office in Chapter 1 with the dope office, floor to ceiling windows, trendy furniture that I visited and was inspired by? The first time I was exposed to what I could achieve as a life coach? Yep, it was him!

I shared with him how I wanted to leave my job to be a Life Coach full time and an adjunct professor but was afraid financially. My current full-time income was my means for paying my bills. We talked about how much revenue would allow me to replace my full-time income - for bills and other necessities. As we continued the conversation, I experienced an *ah-ha* moment, If I taught three classes I would almost be at the income I needed besides the revenue from coaching. By the end of the conversation, I had a plan of what I needed to do to move. The first line of business was to see how much my monthly expenses were. In our conversation, we discussed ballpark numbers, but my first task was to calculate concrete figures. The second task was to contact the Chair of my department to inquire about teaching additional classes.

I am not a person that believes things just happens, but I don't think that week would've led me to that opportunity to create a road map to ditching my full-time job (*by the time you are reading this the plan succeeded*). And the same can happen for you; but you have to take the first step.

What's next for you? Now that you have your vision and you know what you want, it is time to get into action. You will be amazed at what happens once you are honest about what you want. What is one small step you can take to lead you in the direction to make your dream become a reality? For me it was as small as telling the Life Coach what I wanted to accomplish. And then it was emailing to my Department Chair to ask about teaching additional classes. No step is too small.

If living out your dream was as simple as knowing what you want, then this would be where the book ends. Well, but then fear can creep in. Let's discuss how to become aware and identify the fear in your life in Chapter 3.

CHAPTER 3

YOU SCARED, HUH?

"Ready or not, here I come, you can't hide, gonna find you and take it slowly. Ready or not, here I come, you can't hide, gonna find you and make you want me." – The Fugees

"Nothing in life is to be feared, it is only to be understood. Now is the time to understand more, so that we may fear less." – Marie Curie

If you asked me three years ago what I feared, I'd probably would have generated a long list of dangerous animals and other random things. For example, I'm terrified of snakes and spiders. You can readily see these physical, tangible causes of these two fears. They have the potential to be poisonous and bite me. But I recognize that fear has another dimension - the fears we cannot see and that are not based upon any inherent physical danger. These include the fear of: failure, success, inadequacy, and insecurity. These *"fears"* live within our minds, we create internal negative associations with them, and then these manifests in our decisions, choices and actions. I call this "false fear."

How might this show up? Instead of pursuing our dreams, we keep avoiding things, delaying, deferring, making excuses, and procrastinating on tasks or taking action that will get you closer. When you're operating from fear, the time is never right. You may even have someone with a successful track record suggest some concrete Next Steps for you, but you never get started with them. These are just some ways this form of fear can present itself in our lives.

What is Fear?

A basic definition of fear is a distressing emotion aroused by impending danger, evil, pain, etc., whether the threat is real or imagined. When we encounter danger, our physiological response is known as fight our flight. Adrenaline and cortisol hormones are then released to prepare our bodies to either deal with the threat or run away to safety. The issue is that our bodies fail to differentiate between whether it is a real, external danger (*being chased by a ferocious dog*) or a contrived, imagined one (*stepping out of your comfort zone*). The physiological response is similar. Now that we know the basics, how can we identify "*false fear*" within our own lives?

How to Identify "False Fear"

After starting my blog, I felt in my heart I wanted to make by dream real and become a life coach. I noticed that people would often share their aspirations with me and then wanted my input on how they should proceed. I would leave them with actionable steps and support them in being accountable as the days passed. Later they would excitedly return with "*praise reports*" of how they accomplished what they desired to achieve.

I knew this was part of my life mission and I was on fire to do it. However, something went off in me that stopped me dead in my tracks. At first, I could not pinpoint what was keeping me from pursing the life coaching, something to which I seemed to have a natural affinity. It was not until I examined the factors and identified my barriers I moved forward and fulfill my dream of being a life coach for others.

I began by asking myself an important question.

75

If I obtained every resource and the knowledge to pursue this dream, would I do it? My answer was no. I was afraid to call myself a life coach because of how my peers would view me. They didn't have a clear and full understanding about life coaching. In their minds, life coaching was only about sharing motivational quotes all day on social media. Honestly, they would not take me seriously or consider that life coaching was a real profession. Unfortunately, when we don't understand or it's outside of our experience, we judge or place negative labels on it. You're perceived as weird, different, or corny. That is what I was afraid would happen if I staked my claim and *"owned"* being a Life Coach. This *"false fear"* was at the root of me putting on the brakes. And it wasn't until I understood the root cause I could then create a plan to move past it. Where did this fear originate from? Was it something that just appeared in life in that moment or had it always been there?

Discovering the Roots of Your "False Fear"

I have always been a tomboy - a girl who enjoys playing sports, like basketball and football, and carried a strong hate for dresses as a kid. I didn't fit in. The popular girls didn't want to hang out with me; we had nothing in common. And because I was a girl, the boys didn't welcome me into their jock clique with open arms. At recess, I would even bring my own basketball to school in hopes this would increase my chances of being chosen to be on a team with the boys. That plan tanked as they would use my basketball to play and still did not pick me - because I was a girl.

I felt so alone.

Then came 7th grade.

I tried out for my middle school basketball team - and made it! As the only Black person on the team, I became popular overnight! And *everything* changed. I went from being lonely to be the center of attention. During the pep rallies, I would receive the loudest screams when they called my name. People would invite me to sit with them at lunch, and even ask me to hang out with them on the weekends. I finally fit in and have been a part of the cool kid crew ever since.

But I still remember how lonely those elementary school days were though. As I continued to dig deeper, to get at the real root of the reasons behind my hesitation about initially pursuing life coaching, I realized that I didn't want to chase this passion of being a life coach for fear it might threaten the cool kid status I'd had since middle school.

It was over 20 years ago that I went from a "*nobody*" to a popular "*somebody*," and the feelings from that experience resurfaced again to affect my actions. But it wasn't until I sat down to think of when I first felt alone that I connected to my pre-middle school years. I had to look deeper, beyond my situation to discover the source of my fear. From WHAT did this originate? Where did it come from? If I didn't address it, it would continue to interfere with me moving forward.

Now, reflect on your history.

Have results from those events and experiences resurfaced as fear in the present?

_____

_____

_____

_____

For example, did you ever stutter in front of the class and your classmates picked on you now you are deathly afraid to speak in front of groups.

Knowing it is there is one thing but *admitting* that it is preventing you from progressing can be another story. When we refuse to look back, or insist that we are completely fear-free, then that's denial. Let's look into denial.

Denial

We refuse to believe that what is preventing us from reaching our purpose is as simple as a fear that might have been "installed" in our thinking years prior. Since it has been hindering us, we believe that it must be a complicated situation. And we find ourselves in denial; refusing to believe such a thing exists.

It reminds me of the tactics I use when cleaning the house. I hate for random articles of clothing to be draped across the arms of the sofa or a piled in the corner of my room. Anytime that I see clothes draped and piled all over my room drives me crazy! But I also have a strong dislike for getting hangers and placing them on the racks in the closet. To meet my standard of cleanliness and not have to hang them up, I found the perfect solution. If I put them in a pile in the corner of the back of my closet, they are out of my sight and I don't have to hang them up. I trick myself into believing that if the clothes were out of sight, they didn't exist. If the closet door was closed, it meant that the piles of clothes didn't exist! Actually, it wasn't a false solution because I transferred my clothes from one pile, in plain view, to another pile, out of sight in my closet.

We often treat our fears the same way. We think: If I can "*relocate*" them to a place out of my sight, and I don't acknowledge them, that somehow makes it better and they will just evaporate and go away. But time and time again, we've seen this isn't true and it doesn't work this way. So why do we want to believe that "*out of sight is out of mind?*"

If we see it, we must move!

Let's say I didn't have a closet I could pile my clothes in. When I saw it on my sofa, I would be forced to hang it up. Because I couldn't avoid it any longer. To reach my standard of cleanliness (*and it's impossible for me to focus with stuff hanging around*) I would have to do something that otherwise I wouldn't feel like doing. When I acknowledge it (*seeing it lying around*) I would then have to take fitting action (*hang up the clothes*). For you, it may not be clothes scattered around the room but saying phrases such as "*I don't know what to do*" can be a form of avoidance. If I don't know what to do then, well, I can continue to be in denial about the action I can, should or could be taking.

Fear gives off the vibe of a big bad wolf, the bully that teased everyone in elementary school. But when someone stood up to the big bad wolf, he ran like a coward. Fear is not as intimidating as it wants you to believe. Think about the famous Bible Story of David and Goliath. Goliath was the enormous nine-foot warrior who boasted that he could beat any individual in the Israelite army. Then here comes little shepherd boy, David, who pulls out his slingshot and topples Goliath. Using one of the most popular stories from the Bible, let's review the factors that led David to this unlikely victory where all the odds were against him. There is much we can learn from David's story that can empower us in the face of dealing with "*false fear.*"

81

1. David had a Calling

Before we get to the battle, let's look at the events leading to the showdown of David and Goliath. The prophet Samuel was instructed by God to go to the house of Jesse to anoint the next king. The next king was among Jesse's sons. Samuel inspected each of the seven sons that Jesse presented to him. One by one they were all denied. David was out taking care of the sheep; his father Jesse didn't even think enough of him to go get him. Samuel demanded to see him, so Jesse sent for him to come. When David arrived, Samuel 16:12 states *"God said "Upon your feet! Anoint him! This is the one."* David, the son that was a lowly shepherd was selected to be the future king of Israel.

You may believe that your situation has discounted you from what you wish to achieve. How can I pursue my purpose if my bank account is in the negative? I continue to receive rejection letters from every job I apply for, I will never succeed! How can I make an impact if I am always overlooked and undervalued? David was in the field smelly with the sheep; and his dad didn't even think to get him when Samuel arrive. Though his situation wasn't ideal; it did not disqualify

82

him from being anointed as the next king. No matter your situation, you STILL have a purpose on your life.

2. David was obedient

Samuel 17:20 *"And David rose up early in the morning and left the sheep with a keeper and took and went as Jesse had commanded him; and he came to the trench, as the host was going forth to the fight."* Jesse *(David's father)* told David to take food to his brothers who were preparing for battle against the Philistine and to see how they were doing. The next morning David did what he was told. As he approached the camp where his brothers were, the soldiers were preparing to go to battle. While David took the food to his brothers and checked to see how they were doing, Goliath stepped out and shouted his defiance, David heard it. All the Israelites ran in fear. David was wondering why no one was stepping up to fight and inquired to those around him about the reward for killing Goliath. They responded that the king, King Saul, would give great wealth to the man who killed Goliath.

David's oldest brother Eliab, went to David like an overprotective big bro, wondering why he was at the battle field. David was offended because he did nothing but ask a question regarding the reward. Then he inquired with someone else about the reward for killing Goliath. Someone overheard David asking about the reward and reported it to King Saul, who asked for him. When David met King Saul, he then informed him that he would be the one to go fight Goliath.

What if David didn't heed his father's instructions? He would've missed his opportunity to face Goliath. David didn't know that he would be slaying a giant that day; he was simply doing what he was told to do. Saying yes isn't only restricted to a person, but it also applies to a "gut feeling" or a command that God has placed on your heart? You may never know how you are delaying the fulfillment of your purpose because of missing out on the opportunity presenting itself.

One day I was sitting at the University waiting for the office administrator to arrive so I could sign my teaching contract for the upcoming semester. As I waited, a lady sat across from me and we sparked a conversation. When she asked me, what did I do as an occupation, I felt a STRONG tug to tell her that besides being an adjunct professor I was also a blogger and Life Coach. She asked follow up questions about my blog then mentioned that she taught a social media marketing class and would LOVE for me to be a guest speaker for the class to talk about blog creation. I was down! We exchanged information and confirmed the date I would speak.

While I spoke, the class was engaged, they asked great questions, and stayed after to ask additional question, receive help with their blog, and I even had a short coaching session to help one student with the next step on an idea that she had to impact the youth. The professor raved with praises about my talk and asked if I would come speak to her class next semester. Also, she would have a paid opportunity for me to speak to an organization she is the chair of. But that's not all that happened! After I posted about my speech on social media, another professor reached out for me to come speak to his class! Just by following that "*gut feeling*" opened several opportunities for me.

3. David was prepared

In 1 Samuel 17: 33-37, David is having a conversation with King Saul. King Saul is telling David how unqualified he is to fight against Goliath. David was not a warrior, but his past prepared him for this moment. As he kept watch over his sheep, a lion or bear would come and attempt to take one from the herd. David would then go rescue the sheep from the attacker's mouth, and if they got feisty, he would even kill the lion or bear. Though his subject was now a human, if he could defeat those animals, he could come out victorious again.

You may feel you are unqualified to pursue your dream. Though you may not have current experience, your past can equip you to carry out the task. Pause for a moment and think back to the skills of past jobs, organizations you are a part of, or natural abilities. Take an inventory of your skills and abilities by answering these questions to remind you of past skills you can utilize on your journey.

List skills that you have acquired from your work experience?

_____

_____

_____

_____

_____

In what ways have you been able to overcome a challenging moment in your life?

_____

_____

_____

_____

_____

What information or education you have acquired in the past that could be useful?

_____

_____

_____

_____

_____

Don't take anything for granted. We are often more prepared than we perceive ourselves to be.

4. David was authentic

As David prepared to go out to battle, Saul placed his personal suit of armor on him. David realized that he could barely move inside of all this over-sized armor. So, he took the armor off and picked up his shepherd's staff, five smooth stones and his sling. He recognized that, though this armor was perfect for Saul, Saul's armor was not a good fit for him.

What may work great for someone else may hinder you and not be the right fit. Be true to what works for you. Even if someone else continues to talk about how well something may be working for them. It doesn't mean that it's a fit for you; so, take it off!

5. David Acted

David took the sling shot and aimed it towards Goliath's forehead. Down went Goliath. After Goliath lunged at David with his huge spear, he would've been killed instantly if he did not act. Once he moved into action it led to him being victorious.

You can have a million-dollar idea and a thorough business plan; but it means nothing if you do not move into action. You may have a brilliant idea that you will tell anyone with ears about. "I am going to start a non-profit organization that will help the homeless women with children in the city..." You know how it will make an impact, and that it will change lives. However, it is only a fantasy unless you move into action. Your action is what converts the internal thought into external demonstration.

A David resides on the inside of each of us. Though you may believe that you are unqualified, overlooked underestimated, or doubtful; you have all the tools you need, either within you are available outside of you, to take out fear. However, it is now up to you to pick up your slingshot and to sling stones of action, towards your dreams.

Push Through Fear

Pushing through fear can sound simple. Many people will casually just say "*do it.*" Yes, it is a logical answer but when faced with reality, it can be more than a notion. The war is winnable, but you must first conquer the battle in your head. When the presence of fear attempts to make you want to give up on your dreams, to help yourself keep going, ask yourself these questions:

1. What will I gain?

We often view the negative side of what will happen if we attempt our dream. However, we fail to recognize the positive impact that our dreams bring. When I thought about becoming a life coach, I was focused on what people would say instead of all the people I could impact. What you focus on grows, so let's kill the negativity of fear in our dreams.

2. What is my Why again?

This is the perfect time to remind yourself of the reasons to follow through on your dreams. What are you doing it for? The motivation will allow you to press past the fear.

3. What have you overcome?

This is a pat-yourself-on-the-back moment. How have you overcome fear in the past? You once tackled what seemed impossible before and made it! Remind yourself that you can once again win the war with fear. I won the war against fear when I blogged and became a life coach. When I thought about becoming an adjunct professor and fear attempted to discourage me; I had to remind myself of the battles I already won against fear. I remembered how the task wasn't as bad as fear made it sound, and that helped me to reach my goal of becoming an adjunct professor.

4. *What if the worst happens?*

Like me, you may be a little hardheaded and may think of the worst-case scenario. When you think of the worst that can happen, what could you do in response to it? "What if no one buys my product?" "What if no one buys my service?" Well, I could create a survey to see what people want. I could find alternative ways to market my product. What events are my target-market attending? I could promote my services there. This will allow you to handle the anxiety of being prepared if the worst was to happen. Problem solved.

In the Chapter 1, you saw the struggle I was having. I was right there. The time had come where my site was done and all that was left for me to do was to press "*publish*" to put it out into the world. Though it was one action, I felt like a ton of bricks was sitting on my chest. I could barely breathe. It was like finally getting to the front of the line at the amusement park, and then freezing up when it came time to step on to the ride. In that moment, it was like, *"naw, never mind."* After all this time and hard work, I was almost ok with throwing it away. I didn't know what was waiting for me on the other side of pressing *"publish."* Isn't that when fear plays a part in most of our lives? We can freeze up because we have thoughts such as:

How will others respond?

Will they buy it?

Will the loan application from the bank get denied?

What if I fail?

What if I run out of money?

What if I can't handle it?

What if it sucks?

What if I get laughed at, run out of town, and then abducted by aliens?

Because that happens every day, right? It sounds outlandish, but it doesn't stop us from living in the world of *what ifs*. We automatically run to the worse scenario we can think of in our minds. Most of the time those things never happen. So, I will too echo what everyone else says about overcoming fear; get your ass in the seat, pull down the safety bar, and get ready to go on the ride of your life.

5. What if "tomorrow" never comes?

YOLO (you only live once). Seriously, we get one life to live and we don't know when it will end. I use to believe that we all had ample time in life; until I lost classmates, friends, and family members to cancer, health issues, and accidents. As I sat at their funerals, I was reminded that we don't know when the end of our life will be; I would hate to leave this earth with talents and gifts I didn't share because I was afraid or continued to put it off until tomorrow. Each minute is precious because we may not make it to the next. When it is my time to leave this earth, I want to know that I held nothing back and I gave everything that God instructed me to give. That my legacy would live on forever. When I think of my life in that scope the mountain of fear presented in front of me becomes a small molehill I can step over.

Once you tackle those "*false fears*", you still must know where you are going to get on the ride.

CHAPTER 4

THE MAP OF THE PARK

"Setting goals is the first step in turning the invisible into the visible." – Tony Robbins

The amusement park is humongous. Every direction you look there is another ride, attraction, or a food stand, which can lead to feeling overwhelmed or even frustrated. You can see from a distance the roller coaster you want to ride; but how do you find the entrance to ride it? If you don't have a form of guidance to direct you, you may find yourself wandering in circles. Now that you have a picture of what your passion looks like, you may be asking yourself, *"How do I make it happen? What is the best way to guide myself to my desired destination?"* Setting goals can provide you with guidance and also *"stepping stones"* on the way to your destination.

Set Goals

About four years ago, as a grad student, a few friends from home and I took a little trip down to Florida for the weekend. My friend would drive, so I had to meet her at her parents' house. I had only been to her parents' home twice. They stayed across town where I didn't go much so I relied on my phone's GPS to navigate me there both times I went.

But guess what - I dropped my phone in the toilet the day before we were to leave for Florida. Placing it in rice to dry it out didn't resurrect it from phone death, so it was off to Google Maps to print out paper directions. With a packed car and directions in hand, I was ready to hit the road.

My trip to my friend's parents' house was going smoothly, until I missed a turn. I attempted to retrace my steps but continued to miss more turns. Now I had no idea where I was! I was frustrated. None of the streets I passed were correlating with what I had printed out It was early in the morning, so no one was outside to ask for directions. As the minutes passed, nothing around me was familiar and confusion officially set in. And just before I pulled off to the side of the road to sob frantically (*like that was going to help the situation*), I saw a gas station. They would have a phone I could call my friend from. Thank you, GOD! I called her. And after telling her where I was, she guided me to her parent's house. Though I felt very lost, I was just around the corner and could get back on track to arrive to my destination.

In this story my friend's parents' house was my goal, and the step by step instructions was my plan. Though I was lost and got off track, I still met with my friend because I knew my destination. In your life, your destination represents the target of your goals. Now there may be alternate routes for you to take and you may get lost for a while like I did, but fortunately, if you know your destination, you can get back on track.

Start Where You Are

The first question your phone's GPS or Google Maps needs to know when seeking directions is "What is your starting point?" For the device to correctly offer various solutions it must first know where you are – your current location. Where are you? What is your location? Not in the physical sense but in relation to the goals you set out to achieve. Here are some questions to get you started:

- What current resources do I have access to?
- What can I invest financially now?

- What knowledge I possess that can I leverage?

- What needs am I equipped to fulfill or can equip myself to fulfill?

- What research can I do to increase my "IQ" in this area?

- What marketable and monetizable gifts, talents, and skills do I offer?

- Who has expertise in this field with a successful track record that can be a resource?

I realized that I knew nothing about blogging before I started my blog. I had a basic knowledge of the blogging world. After answering and assessing the seven questions above, I recognized from where I was starting. I knew that my first step needed to be to research information about how to start a blog. I went to a resource I knew would have all the basic answers: Google. During my research I found options for blog platforms to use, how to create blog posts, and how to write captivating headlines.

As I began my research, I realized how important it was to know the focus of my blog and to be clear about who my audience, my ideal reader, would be. My second step to create my ideal reader became clear once I took my first step to research about blogs. Side note: when following directions from a GPS, it gives you one direction at a time, sequentially. It doesn't move you on to the next step in the directions until you complete the first one. You may be hung up because you are at the starting point and the steps you need to take have not yet presented themselves. It takes for you to take the first step and then what needs to be done next will be more apparent and readily recognizable to you. Once I knew how to create a blog post and understood my target audience, I then sat down and started writing.

Think of it this way. *What do you want to accomplish? Then ask what resources or person(s) could lead you to knowing a step to take?* A step is one action. Don't fulfill on your goal in one day. It is a step that takes you that much closer to understanding what you will need to accomplish your goal. And I also recommend writing down your goal and the steps to your goal.

Did you know that people who develop goals are more likely to achieve what they set out to do versus those who don't? Dr. Gail Matthews, a psychology professor at the Dominican University in California

99

conducted a study and found that subjects of the study were 42% more likely to achieve their goals by creating and writing them down. The Reticular Activating System (RAS), which is located at the stem of your brain, filters urgent information from your conscious mind and sends it to your subconscious mind. This information now seeps within your subconscious only to resurface later. When you write down your goals, it activates additional neural pathways within your brain that allow you to visualize and develop images. Your RAS will then bring to your attention people, situations, and circumstances which can bring them to life. When possible, solutions come into your space, you will notice them. But there are guidelines to remember with effective goal setting that will support your progress and success. Below you will find guidelines to follow that will guide you as you create your own goals.

Be Realistic

Stretching yourself is a great idea; however, creating goals that require a unicorn to appear, and a genie to grant you three wishes may not work. You don't just wake up one day and it is completed. You want to develop goals that stretch you but that are still possible to reach with the resources available to you. When we develop unrealistic goals, it allows us to purchase a one-way ticket to being disappointed. For example, unrealistic would look like starting a YouTube channel and wanting to have ten thousand subscribers on the first day. A realistic goal would be to obtain 200 subscribers in your first week.

Be Specific

The goal shouldn't be too general but articulated so it makes the results measurable. A goal to become a successful million-dollar business man or woman is cool; but developing a brand to generate $5,000 by the end of your first year is a more obtainable and identifiable goal. In addition, if there is no timeframe set, it is a wish and not a goal.

Set a Timeframe

Give a time by which you aim to complete your goal(s). If you do not give your goal a time to be completed, other task that aren't urgent will take priority and you also can procrastinate. Otherwise, it's easy to slip into thinking: I'll do it tomorrow. And then tomorrow turns into weeks, months, even years. Instead of a general intention such as I want to launch a blog; update it to, I want to launch a blog in three months and have an actual date set that reflects the launch date.

Now that you know how to state a goal, let's develop an action plan to work towards it.

Break It Down

Your goal may take you six months to a year to accomplish, or longer, depending on the goal. It takes implementing smaller tasks and purposeful actions each day or week. It may take weeks or months to fulfill on the plans and action items that support the fulfillment of a goal. Break your goal down into "bite-size" chunks so that you're clear about each next step you need to take. Let's work towards your goals.

Answer these questions as they will assist you in developing goals, 90 days at a time, and the action steps you can take today and going forward.

THE MAP OF THE PARK

What is a goal you would like to fulfill?

_____

_____

_____

_____

_____

_____

What is a step you will take TODAY to move you closer to your goal?

_____

_____

_____

_____

_____

_____

What is a supporting action you can establish and complete by the end of THIS WEEK that will allow you to draw closer to your dream?

_____

_____

_____

_____

_____

What is a supporting action you can complete NEXT WEEK that will allow you to draw closer to your goal?

_____

_____

_____

_____

_____

What is your 30-day objective?

_____

_____

_____

_____

_____

_____

What is your 60-day objective?

_____

_____

_____

_____

_____

_____

What is your 90-day objective?

_____

_____

_____

_____

_____

Okay, so now it's time to put this into practice. Time to get into action! Put the book down right now. Look at what you wrote for the first question. Go complete that task right now (*or at least START*), and then come back and continue reading. Now that you have a plan in place; let's address how to navigate distractions that will try to stray you from achieving your goal.

My Weak Spot

Amusement parks will try every tactic to lure you into spending every dime you have on you. After paying to park, the entry ticket has a price tag. You may think that after dishing out those coins, your debit card can go back into your wallet. Well, not so soon, buddy. Then there are souvenir shops with countless baubles and "shiny objects," then clothes that are often so gimmicky that they should never be worn in public. Then there's the carnival style games you have a .05% chance of winning, and then the arm and leg they charge for food and drinks.

I do an awesome job of bypassing on all the above, but one thing gets me every time – the FUNNEL CAKES! This delicious treat is made of cake batter that is poured through a funnel into hot grease. Once removed powdered sugar is then sprinkled on top. I swear, there is some type of drug in the batter. As soon as the sweet aroma hits my nose, I must go find it. I track it down like a bloodhound. I walk around the park like a K-9 dog searching for a criminal when that funnel cake aroma hits my nose. Funnel cakes have the power to throw me off track and override my original plans.

So Easily Distracted

Distractions can throw you off your game. The ride you were looking for may be just around the corner, but now you get off course looking for some funnel cakes. And you're on a diet, so shouldn't even be eating them in the first place - but you can't resist. Instead of staying on track with the action steps that support the fulfillment of your dreams, you get thrown off or lured off-course by distractions.

Consider this......Before I wrote this book, I sat down and created a date by which I wanted to complete my first draft. All set up and ready to write, I had a notification from the social media photo sharing app Instagram. As I checked to see what it was, people were liking my latest post; but there was a username that I did not recognize. As I clicked on the profile and this man was fine! Now I must look and find all his social media profiles to see if *he is in a relationship, married, had kids, acceptable occupation, and goes to church? Does he love his mama? (You will be surprised at what you can find out about a person through their social media profiles).* As I wrap up my "*investigation*," I glance at the clock. *What??!?!* The two hours I was supposed to devote to working on this book were spent on sleuthing about this man! Distracted! That day, he was my "funnel cake."

Most of us have some type of *"funnel cake"* in our lives we find difficult to pass up. We allow it to throw us off our game and take us off-focus. Here are some things to remember when you feel the urge to chase the sweet aroma of funnel cakes.

Willpower Isn't Enough

There is tons of noise and over-stimulation in our society and everyone is jockeying for our attention. The question becomes: how can we block it out and do what we need to do to stay focused? Often, the answer is *"I need to have more willpower."* Willpower is over-rated. We're often told that with every distraction will power can win out. But it doesn't. It works much like a knife. The first time you use it on a steak it cuts with no issues. Overtime if it is not sharpened, it gets more and more dull, and you may struggle to get it through a steak. And most of us believe that we possess a "new knife" level of willpower, but have a dulled willpower. Relying on powering through it alone with your willpower alone is a recipe for disaster in the making. Instead try out the tactics below to assist you with conquering distractions.

Set Limits

If you think about it, working for five hours straight sounds productive. Think about all the tasks you could complete if you had five hours of uninterrupted time. *Now come back to reality.* Think about a Saturday in which you have nothing planned on the calendar. You think to yourself, *"Wow I'm going to get so much done today."* Because your time seemed abundant, you accomplished less since you had no timelines. You weren't focused.

Journalist and author, Tony Schwartz reported that we are most productive in smaller spurts, around 90-minute windows. Be focused and in purposeful action for 90 minutes at a time, then take a brief break, and get back to it. The break allows you to rejuvenate instead of pounding yourself to burnout As I took this approach, I found I actually accomplished more and I had more energy doing it. It is like working for a treat. Get through those 90 minutes and I then can enjoy a little distraction without feeling guilty because I worked for it. And it also allows my brain a break so thoughts get a

refreshment break and I'm not forcing a solution to what
I am working on. The short break allows me to gather
new ideas to a problem that could otherwise have been
dragged out for days.

Be Smarter

We can't rely solely on will power; make smarter choices.
If you know that TV is your main "*funnel cake*," then why,
oh why, would you sit in front of the television when
you know there are some specific dream-supporting
tasks you need to complete? Be smarter about it! Ask
yourself: *"What can I do to redirect my attention back to my
dream work?"* If that means you must turn off your TV
and unplug the cable box, or leave your phone in another
room, locked in a box, turned off altogether, on silent,
or in the back of the closet, do it. But don't allow the
aroma of the "funnel cake" to distract you and keep you
from getting on the ride.

Time is Ticking

Slackin' is a dangerous habit to form. Don't even get me
started on becoming lazy or too comfortable. I know the
feeling- when the seat conforms perfectly to your booty,

and there is a marathon of your favorite show on TV. Whew! It's nearly impossible to pull yourself away and get up. And though you know you have things to get done, you rationalize.

"Oh, I'll do it tomorrow."

Then "tomorrow" never comes.

It's easy to get caught up at the amusement park especially when you enjoy the sport of people watching. Back in the day some friends and I were at the park. We decided to take a potty break after a ride. One friend did not have to go to the restroom so he sat down on a park bench. After we each finished our business, we joined him and waited for everyone else to come out.

After the whole crew was there, it seemed as if every person that walked by gave us something to talk about. Conversations about others turned into stories; which flipped into more conversations and stories. This was only supposed to be a maximum five-minute bathroom break, but we became comfortable and the day passed us by. The plan we had to get on more rides was now dead and gone.

111

Initially, in our lives, we can start with these high aspirations, only to sit down *"on a bench"* and get so comfortable that we lose track of time and forget that we had other stuff to do. The purpose wasn't to go to the amusement park to sit around and talk; we could've done that at home *for free*. The purpose of going to the park was to get on the rides. In our lives, we can get too comfortable, and we settle. We allow ourselves to lose sight of the goal. What would only be a quick pit stop turns into a lengthy time-waster.

When we do this, we stay in our pit stop way longer than intended. It can be discouraging and give us just enough time to plant a Doubt Seed. It can make us believe that we are meant to stand still instead of experiencing all that life should offer. Don't get me wrong, pit stops are necessary. However, don't become content with the pit stop becoming a permanent situation. *Will you stay on the park bench, or get up and get on the ride?* You may also waste your time by comparing yourself to others.

Comparisons

Comparing yourself to others is a big time-waster and

useless "on the bench" activity. You are especially susceptible to this with social media. Recognize these scenarios?

Logs on to Facebook - *as you read through other's posts, you think to yourself....*

"What? She just got engaged?! Well, but me and my boo been together longer than them!"

"He just got a new job; he's not even that smart!"

"Dang, we graduated together and she's now speaking at the White House...really?!"

"How'd she gets 400 likes on that? Her Instagram caption is not even that deep!"

Oh buddy, social media is a dangerous entrapment zone for comparison. Though it's used to keep up with folks, it usually leaves the door open to see too much of their lives; and typically, usually only the best stuff. So, it's easy to grade our entire lives up against the highlight reel they share with us.

Here's an analogy from track and field that also

applies. Coaches tell their athletes to keep their eyes on the finish line and to stay in their lane. First, because the moment they step outside of the white line, they are disqualified. But what I love to see is a neck and neck race. I mean, one of them where you don't know who will take it all. The crowd is up and everyone is screaming *"MOVE, MOVE, MOVE"* *(in track terms that means go FASTER!).* As they approach the end of the race, it never fails; one runner becomes curious to see how far the others are from them. As soon as they turn to look, the energy it took to turn their heads gave the person the tenth of a second to get ahead.

The same thing happens to us. When we shift our focus from our efforts, even a little bit, and look around to compare where we are related to others, we can set ourselves up for a defeat. What would happen if you minded your own business instead of worrying about what is happening in someone else's Kool-Aid?

The plot twist is that you may be doing well in life; but then you compare your picture to all or parts of theirs. We can then beat ourselves up and begin an imaginary competition. A social media war that only you know about. It becomes about how many *"likes"* your picture can get. How many *"shares"* you can get, or how many *"views"* your video received. This creates an unhealthy, obsessive competition that can be damaging.

I once conversed with a friend about a YouTube channel they wanted to start. When I asked her how things were going, she went on a tangent about another YouTube star. She was ranting about how this YouTuber was younger than her, had thousands of followers on Instagram, and generated enough revenue to quit her full-time job. When my friend compared herself to this YouTuber, it left her feeling discouraged, agitated, jealous and disempowered. She hadn't even gotten her YouTube channel started. What if she pointed out how impressed she was with this other person instead, or even reached out to her for advice or to interview her about her journey to quitting her job? This would have created a very different response within her. Comparison will leave you feeling defeated, deflated, and often, frustrated.

This is tough to overcome. The culture has created social media comparison machines - a generation that just wants to *"put on for the 'gram"* (*Instagram, that is*). When you come across a certain person's profile, you can say things to yourself such as, *"Why she is getting all these likes; she's not even that dope."* We can become very judgmental and pick the other person apart. If this is describing you, my friend, even if just a little bit, then you have a case of Comparison Disease. Here is your prescription - take an extended break from social media. This means no checking, or posting for at least 10 days. Yes, that means a 10-day social media *"fast,"* where you abstain from social media for 10 days. Instead practice gratitude. When you wake up, write down three specific things or experiences that you're grateful for from your previous day. This allows you to give energy and attention to your blessings. Gratitude researcher Robert A. Emmons, also found that practicing gratitude reduces toxic emotions such as frustration and regret, increases happiness, and decreases depression. People who practice gratitude can also appreciate other people's accomplishments instead of being resentful or jealousy. Water your own grass instead coveting or obsessing over someone else's.

Change your Focus

Social media consistently reminds us of what somebody else is doing. How can we shift that focus with so many images and messages bombarding us on social media? It sounds easy to do. But, it's hard to stop drifting over into someone else's lane and getting our attention tangled up in somebody else's business or life - Somebody that isn't even thinking about you. And they might not even know who you are!

I do this when I lose focus. I bring my attention back to the goals I have set and my reasons for wanting to accomplish them. This keeps me reminded of MY goals and dreams. Then I look at how I can invest in myself. Before we discussed if you are experiencing "*comparison disease*" to go on a social media fast. If social media is DISTRACTING you, find ways to limit your social media consumption. You will be focused on yourself and not others. It limits distractions. At what time of the day will you check social media for business? Could you utilize social media posting sites such as Hootsuite or Buffer to automate your postings to limit your social media use?

News Flash: Social media, if not used constructively, can be your downfall. It can be a tripwire that undermines you fulfilling on your dream. If

you remember nothing else in this book, I want you to remember this point.

So, let's flip the script, and look at how limiting or abstaining (for a period of time) from social media can be a huge benefit to you. When I cut cable (*which I will discuss later in the chapter*) I also cut social media for an entire month. I was productive because I wasn't checking my social every hour to see how many likes a picture received. And I actually had to call and text friends to see how they were doing instead of assuming from their social media post. Some other benefits from limiting social media are: reduce FOMO (*fear of missing out*), live in the moment (*instead of taking pictures and recording events to post on social*), improve your mood (*research shows that social media has been linked to depression*).

In what ways could limiting social media benefit you?

_____

_____

_____

_____

_____

THE MAP OF THE PARK

What could you do with the time you direct AWAY from social media and TO another useful task?

_____

_____

_____

_____

_____

When you conquer distractions, you can give your focus to the actions that will bring you closer to fulfilling your dream. It will also assist you in making the right choices when faced with a decision.

Aligned Action

You will be presented with choices daily. During a typical day, studies show that we're making hundreds of choices – which clothes to wear, which radio station to listen to while we commute to work, what to eat for lunch, what task to do first, etc. We can either make choices that take us to the funnel cake or choices that keep us moving towards the ride. I like to refer to the walk towards the ride as aligned action. Aligned actions are the choices you make and the actions you take that are line with your goal.

Back when I still had cable TV, I enjoyed nothing more than TGIT, *"Thank God it's Thursday."* It is what the ABC TV network calls its Thursday night line- up. Shonda Rhimes wrote and produced all three hit TV shows that aired on Thursday nights - *Grey's Anatomy, Scandal, and How to Get Away with Murder (HTGAWM).* Out of the three, Scandal and HTGAWM were MY shows! ABC could have placed me on their pay roll for all the people I made watch and love those shows.

While I was building my blog, I was also working two jobs. The time I had available was slim, so every minute of my calendar counted if I wanted to make things happen. TV was a huge part of how I was spending my time, so I decided to only watch TV on the weekends. I gained back hours of time each week with this decision. That way I could accomplish more during the week. Mondays, Tuesdays, and Wednesdays were a breeze - this sacrifice thing wasn't so bad. But oh, buddy when Thursday night at 9:00pm rolled around, and the season premiered, *would I fall victim to TGIT or engage in aligned action?* You're probably thinking it was only a show, and that I could watch it the next day. Chile, do you know what could happen on just one episode? Since I persuaded those around me to watch it, they were crazy about it and it was the popular topic of discussion.

At first it was hard, especially when I would come across spoiler alerts (*when an important detail about the show is revealed while browsing social media*). Someone would hint at the juicy details of what had happened on a most recent episode, and then I would be itching to know what happened. On Scandal, did Fitz and Olivia get back together for the 3,984,032th time? In HTGAWM, who did Annalise and her students kill this time? So many questions I needed answered. I had a burning desire to watch, but had to ask myself, "A*re these shows more important than my dreams? I'm watching actors and actresses fulfill their dreams, but while I'm watching them, is it helping me fulfill mine?*" It was a hard decision, but a necessary one. I needed to get where I wanted to be.

Once I cut weekly TV out of the equation, I gained on average a whopping 12 hours a week. Yes, TWELVE WHOLE HOURS! I could plan the content I wanted to write over the month and complete those posts; write guest blogs for other sites to grow my following and read a book a week. Because I was not watching TV before bedtime, I even slept better. Before cutting out weekly TV-watching, I would lie down in the bed and it would take me over an hour to fall sleep. But now, because it was quiet before bedtime and TV had been deleted from my weekly routine, my mind was clear, and I would fall asleep within minutes of going to bed.

Since I maximized my time, it allowed me to be productive and do things that previously I said I didn't have time for. This included being involved in the young adult ministry at church and becoming an adjunct professor at Johnson C. Smith University. Besides my new-found productivity, I also saved more money. It didn't make sense to pay a $187 cable bill and only watch TV on the weekends, so I discontinued my cable and kept my internet. It saved me over $137 a month. Do the math - that is around $1,600 a year and $6,500 over the last four years! One aligned action can create a flood of benefits. And here's the kicker - on the weekends I can still watch all my shows I didn't watch during the week on streaming services such as Netflix and Hulu, so I never missed a beat!

You want to notice what you consider as

priorities by looking at what you spend your time on. Is there a disconnect between what you want to achieve and where you are putting your time? What aligned action should you make today? Remember that focusing on what supports your dreams may be seemingly inconvenient for a season, but the positive benefits of that decision will last well beyond the moment, and the impact might even be for a lifetime.

But the moment you get close, there may be another obstacle you didn't see coming.

CHAPTER 5

GETTING OUT OF

YOUR OWN WAY

"Just imagine how much you'd get done if you
stopped actively sabotaging your own work"
– Seth Godin

The moment was around the corner. I can almost see it. The launch of my blog was less than a month away. I was close to posting my first product. Maybe your YouTube video only needs a couple more edits until it is ready, or you're putting the finishing touches on a new product or service before the "big reveal." Your idea is close to being released out into the world. This anticipation is much like seeing the roller coaster's entrance and being only a few people away from "Next" while you wait in line with antsy anticipation.

Finally, you are approaching the ride's entrance. The line is wrapped around to the outside of the gate. The screams of the riders penetrate your ears-as you also observe the look of both thrill and fright on their faces.

It sinks in and the moment becomes real for you. *It's about to happen.* As you prepare to get in line, you experience a range of emotions. On one hand you're excited, the joy of moving fast and furious gives you a high; but in that same breath the emotions associated with a new and possibly scary experience freak you out. Your mind starts to self-sabotage your thoughts. You think to yourself...

I can always catch this ride next time.

The sign says don't ride if you have back pain. My back was giving me issues earlier in the week.

This is not such a good idea;

I should just chill out and pass on this.

    Though there are many obstacles we can face, unfortunately we can wonder *"Am I qualified to be here?"* and our knees can shake. We can talk ourselves out of our blessing. We can get "cold feet" as we edge closer and closer to something becoming REAL. In other words, we can self-sabotage our own destiny right as we near the point of "launch time" or it becomes real.

125

THE ROLLER COASTER EFFECT

What causes us to do this self-sabotage thing? Psychologist Ellen Hendriksen reports there are five reasons for this:

1. Self-Worth: We don't feel we deserve success or happiness. This feeling of unworthiness is connected to cognitive dissonance. It is when our thoughts and actions are out of sync with our beliefs and values. If we experience success but still see ourselves as being worthless, we will halt, undermine or sabotage our achievement to get rid of the dissonance.

2. Control: We would rather be in control of our failure rather than be surprised or blindsided by it. If something bad will happen we'd rather have control of it rather than spinning out of control.

3. Perceived Fraudulence: Have you heard of the term "impostor syndrome?" It is when we believe that if we continue to experience success, more than likely we will be found to be a fake. We can feel like a phony.

4. Familiarity: If you feel you have always been overlooked, mistreated, or exploited, you will default to choosing familiarity over contentment. It is more

familiar and reassuring to place yourself back in that position.

5. Sheer boredom: Sabotaging ourselves can provide our bodies with a rush. If things are going well, we may pick a fight or create drama to experience that rush of adrenaline. *"Sabotaging ourselves creates the familiar feeling of instability and chaos."*

While reviewing the reasons and the different ways we tend to self-sabotage ourselves, were any of them sound familiar? If the answer is yes, can you see how it may be linked to a fear you may be putting in your own way?

When it Doesn't Go Wrong...

Over the years, love relationships have been a sour spot for me. Unhealthy relationships had become a norm for me. For him to lie, cheat, and refuse to commit was just another walk in the park for me. I became so numb to the feeling that when I dated a guy that proved to be different, I became uneasy. He differed from the rest, but I just knew that one day he would show his true colors. But as the relationship continued to develop, it

127

didn't happen. He continued to be a great guy, which should be a breath of fresh air for me, right?

But it wasn't.

It's crazy that the very thing I yearned for was happening. I should have been embracing the moment. I should have been thankful, excited, thrilled. But *what do you do when nothing goes wrong and things are going RIGHT?* Silly to think about it, but we can sometimes brace ourselves for what we *don't* want; we anticipate a detour, a disappointment or a delay. Since the relationship didn't seem to be naturally tanking, as they usually did, I found a way to make it go wrong. I informed him I didn't have the time to develop or feed a relationship right now. So, I broke it off with him. In my mind, I was freaking out. I mean, it was just too good to be true... or was it? When situations don't go wrong, we will search or create a way to end our progress.

Over a year later, I did some reflection on how I treated him. I realized, after the fact, that I was wrong for not giving him a fair chance. And you better believe it when I told my girls I stopped talking to him for no reason, they gave me a major side eye. Though we didn't get back together, after apologizing for my actions, we became great friends. The lesson I learned was that I missed out on the possibility of what could've been a great relationship. But I didn't get to experience it because I had been hurt, and I actually was attempting to protect myself from experiencing heartbreak again.

A False Sense of Effort

We can become pros at creating failure, and don't even know it. Example: You are bummed that no one is purchasing your products, but you have yet to market your products properly. I had a friend who said she wanted to land her dream job, and was not getting a call back for interviews. But she had applied to 85 jobs with the *same* resume and cover letter! Yet she continued to be surprised when she landed no interviews. Putting forth a little *"effort"* may make it *appear* that you are doing something, but it may not be aligned with what you say you want or you're not putting the effort in the right place. You may be putting forth the effort and taking actions, but they are not moving you any closer to your desired goal or outcome because they are out of line. Beneath all the effort and activity, you may actually be scared that

129

you may get what you asked for.   It could challenge your sense of worthiness and deservingness to consider that this could really happen for you. That's enough to scare folks to death. Psychologist Gay Hendricks refers to it as an "Upper Limit" problem – the internal glass ceiling we don't realize that we've set for ourselves that prevents us from living to the fullest. Are your "*false fears*" or negative belief patterns preventing you from putting forth the effort to see results?

It's Not About You

We can mentally create issues with others. It's like walking down the street and you see someone whispering. Then you automatically believe that they are whispering about you. Then you second guess all that you were once confident about before you left the house. We can make a whole lotta nothin' into something sometimes, then we wonder why drama or dysfunction always seems to find us. If we're used to struggling, "*efforting*," forcing, pushing, controlling or trying to "*make*" it happen, peace can be unfamiliar, even foreign, and you may look to bring back the feeling you are accustom to – chaos or confusion. If this is your "*m. o.*," then when life becomes peaceful, subconsciously we can feel the urge to shake things up and create struggle or difficulty for ourselves.

The Four Agreements by Don Miguel Ruiz changed my outlook and helped me understand how I was creating issues and challenges for myself. One agreement is, *"Don't take anything personally."* Ruiz explains,

> *"Nothing others do is because of you. What others say and do is a projection of their own dream. When you are immune to the opinions and actions of others, you won't be the victim of needless suffering."*

Have you ever created a story in your head about a situation, only to find that all the elements of the version of things in your head were based on your presumptions and not on fact? This happened when I was dating the previous guy I mentioned. He had given me no reason not to trust him, but on this day I called him after I left work as I usually did. No answer. Twenty minutes later I sent him a text; no answer. *Oh, so he's just not going to answer his phone, huh. I bet he is out with another girl! Wow, is he going to cheat on me like this?!* And then an hour later, he called me back. When I answered the phone, with my panties all in a bunch, I was ready to let him know that I was not the one to be played with. Well, that was until I could hear the sleep in his voice as he was taking a nap when I called him. My translation of Don Miguel Ruiz agreement is to *stop creating and believing fake stories.* Stop filling in the blanks with your own speculation, which can be exaggerated, flat out wrong, or incorrect. It usually leads to hurt, worry, or both.

And this agreement also applies when people say harmful things to your face. Their words often have nothing to do with you personally. Yes, it can sting but don't allow it to throw you off of your square because it has more to do with *them* than it does with you. It could their insecurities or projections of their own self-perceived inadequacies.

Embrace Being Alone

Earlier, I alluded to my fear of the dark. I am terrified to be somewhere that is pitch black. So, one Wednesday night I was at Bible Study in the meeting room of our church. I try to drink a gallon of water daily to stay well-hydrated. So, this night, my bladder was filled to the brim. I had to use the bathroom and use it bad! As I rose from my seat, our Bible Study leader informed me

I would have to use the alternative bathroom, because the doors were locked to the one we usually used.

No prob, Bob, I thought to myself.

I went to the other side of the room where the door connected to the Fellowship Hall. I knew where I needed to go; through this room and then the other bathroom was in the hallway on the opposite side of the Hall. To my surprise, I opened the door to see only blackness - it was pitch black! Only thing you could see was the dimly lit "Exit" sign above the doorway that led to the bathroom. As I stood there contemplating the long, dark journey (at least it seemed that way.) through the Fellowship Hall, I freaked out.

I popped back into our meeting room, frightened and harried but still attempting to keep my cool. Everyone in Bible Study all gave me the confused look; *Did Jas just see a ghost? Did you actually see Jesus at the altar getting his praise on?*

I told them it was dark, and I couldn't see. Truth was - I was scared. I wouldn't be able to see what was in front of me *(even though there was nothing in my path to harm me)*. I mean, you never know, right? The boogie man could be in there ready to kidnap me. Being alone in the midst of even these few feet of darkness had me shaking in my boots. I sat there uncomfortable for the rest of the night. My bladder was to the brim, but I would not walk through that dark room. Was I this afraid of the dark I was willing to possibility pee on myself? It wasn't just the dark. It was that I would be ALONE.

There is power in having time by yourself. However, in our pop culture, where we venerate constantly being in motion and getting our value from being around others, society sometimes views doing things alone as a downfall. In this you–must-be-doing-something-every-moment-of-every-minute society, spending time by yourself and with yourself can have negative connotations, or maybe mean that you're a loner. We must realize that we sometimes need to separate to elevate.

I remember college and the cafeteria. The cafeteria was only open during certain times for breakfast, lunch, and dinner. With a busy class schedule, club meetings, and athletics, it was a full day. And me and my group of friends all seemed to be on different schedules. But there was always that one friend who had free time and could not find anyone to eat with her. Instead of going to grab something to eat, and sitting in the cafeteria without "*the crew*," she didn't eat. She would rather go hungry than eat alone. Are we that afraid of being alone that we will even go hungry instead?

I have lost count of all the females who have cut their eyes at me because I suggested that they go to the movies alone. What is it that scares us so much about this proposition? And I've noticed that my female friends are the ones that have this "*fear of being alone*" the worst. What are we afraid of confronting? What are we making it mean? Are we running away from the thought of being alone with our own thoughts, with our own energy, with our own presence? If we are consistently around others, or always looking at screens (*phone, TV, computer, the movies*), our mind is in Talk Mode or Entertainment Mode. We think we must entertain our friends, or we're in a passive state of not thinking because we're watching something and being entertained. And it gives us a reason not to be present or with our own thoughts.

Separation from outside stimuli allows us to get back in tune with ourselves and face issues that have been circulating in our heads. The opinions and

135

thoughts of others can cloud our perceptions, and have us always seeking answers outside of ourselves, but Alone Time can give you mental space to sort things out and get clear. You can "*hear yourself think*" and distinguish your own thoughts and determine which are from you which are not your own. Alone Time can also help you become aware of situations in which you attempt to self-sabotage your journey. Besides going places by yourself you can also journal (*which I will provide writing prompts in Chapter 11*), reading (*a book list is in Chapter 7*), participating in a creative project on Pinterest, taking a bath, or going for a walk outside.

My Alone Time involves riding in the car in silence. My commute to work is typically 45 minutes. I turn my music or any podcasts off. I use this Alone Time to think without any distractions. I can have a problem I have been attempting for days to find a solution for, but after experiencing the silence, it seems to drop in my head!

Be careful not to add to the obstacles that may prevent your progress. After reading this chapter look for the signs of how self-sabotage may be popping up in

your life and handle it cordially. It is time to get out of
your own way; your dreams are counting on you!

CHAPTER 6

THE POWER OF INFLUENCE

"If all your little friends jump off a cliff, are you going to jump, too?" – My mama

Your crew. Your tribe. Your besties. Your ride or dies.

…also known as your friends.

Our friends play a key role in our time at the amusement park. Have you ever gone over to a friend's house and had the time of your life? No entertainment or no drinks to have you "*turnt up,*" just you and your friends? When the right people are around you, you can have a great time no matter the situation and without relying on alcohol or drugs to alter your mood or bring on a certain mood. Imagine the same hang out with a whack crew. You would be watching the clock, or scheming up a fake emergency so you have a reason to cut out early *(you text a friend and ask her to call you in five minutes and say she needs you to pick her up…you know how it goes).*

A lot of time is spent at the amusement park

waiting in long lines. But if your friends are entertaining and y'all have a good time with each other the time will fly by. You will be too busy enjoying the moment, having fun and not watching the clock.

Why are the right friends so important?

Let me sum it up for you in one word:

INFLUENCE.

The power of influence is something I didn't understand until I got older, although I had heard it often as a child. My older cousin had a group of questionable friends. My grandmother always told her she needed to watch who she was hanging with. She told her that her friends weren't true friends. The only time she would miss curfew was when she was with them. When she would hang with them, her grades would drop, and she got into trouble in school. However, she was close to being an angel child when they weren't around.

All this time I just thought that my grandma was a hater. *Grandma, let her have a good time with her crew; stop cramping her style,* I would think to myself. At that young age, I didn't understand the influence friends have on us. I was a naïve seven-year-old. I didn't understand. Your friends would never do anything to get you in trouble, right? They would always think about your best interest, right? Why would someone who was your friend tell you to do something that would get you in trouble?

Influence is when someone can affect someone's behavior. Because of the bond you may have with your friends and your desire for acceptance or to fit in, you may partake in activities you wouldn't necessary do by yourself - good or bad. If your friends work out, you may be open to going to the gym more. Have you ever used certain slang or words your friends use without thinking much about it?

That made me think. Why is that friends have this influence over us? I mean, we pick up some things from our family, too; but who do we see ourselves mimicking? If someone is cool, I coin them my *"friend."* And if I don't want to rock with them anymore, I can throw them the deuces with little obligation. We don't have a choice in who family is, but we DO have a choice in who our friends are.

140

When we connect with our crew, it is usually a result of similar characteristics - birds of a feather do flock together. So, when they fly in another direction, more than likely, you will change course to follow them. How we chose our friends also involves how we perceive ourselves. We hang with those whom are like us - have common interests, similarities, or we just vibe well. But also, we can choose our friends based on what we feel we are missing. You may not be funny but like to hang around funny people. Again, it is based on your self-perception of how you see yourself.

Watch who you surround yourself with. They will either help boost you to where you want to go like wind beneath your wings or drag you down or keep you down like a heavy weight on your ankle.

The Power of Peer Pressure

Before college I never had the desire to drink alcohol. But the fad was to get drunk and come back to school and tell everybody how turned up you were. My mother is sweet but can get a little crazy; and I don't believe she was scared to go to jail for beating down her teenage girl for drinking. I didn't want those problems, so I stayed

141

clear of alcohol.

Well, that was until I was hanging out with a couple of friends one night. One of them had gotten their hands on some Smirnoff wine coolers; and then preceded to hand me one. *"Nah, I'm good, I don't drink,"* I said. Oh, *why* did I say that? A flood gate of persuasion occurred...

"Come on Jas, don't be lame."

"So, you just going to be the only person not to drink?"

"I promise you that you don't want to miss out on this stuff...it's so good."

I didn't want to be the odd ball out of the group. I didn't want to "look square," I didn't want to risk being alienated by my friends, so I folded. If I was by myself and that bottle of Smirnoff was sitting there, I wouldn't have been in the least interested in taking a swig. But the influence and pressure from my friends persuaded me do it *(Well, some of the blame belongs to me. Don't go around blaming your friends for everything - you play a part as well).*

142

THE POWER OF INFLUENCE

But what if we had a crew to influence us to choose positive action, or to do something of greater good? My friends, who are more like sisters, have influenced me through their support. They know that I love to read, so my friend Cherrelle randomly bought me a book. She included a note in the book that almost brought me to tears. It read, "You have been an inspiration to me and others. Never let your work go in vain! Always fight for your dreams. I believe in you." I place that note right above my desk, and in those moments when I felt defeated or questioned the value I am offering, I looked at that note. And Daphnie, who is an author of two children's books, knew that I had been stalled working on this book. She purchased me a book entitled "Today is the Day." This book is all about sharing your God-given purpose with the world. My friends also speak life. For a birthday gift my friend Dymond purchased me a cup that read "World's Greatest Life Coach" and on the shipping label she put "World Renowned Author & Life Coach, Jasmine Hill." They continue to push me and remind me of the gift I have to share with the world. And for that, I am forever grateful! The accomplishments we would reach would be astonishing because we're not operating on just our own

143

inspiration and determination alone! This is why you want to have friends with these five characteristics.

Top Five

It was a beautiful Saturday around one or two in the afternoon. This is peak lazy time for me and I was partaking in every minute. Though I had tons of tasks to complete, I opted to sit on the couch and watch endless hours of *Good Times (the 70's sitcom about the Evans family in the projects of Southside Chicago, also known as the best show ever, to me at least)*. I have watched all six seasons at least a hundred times, and on this Saturday, I was gunning for one hundred and one. I snuggled into the corner of the couch eating a bag of Cheetos. It seemed as if I would be stuck in that spot for a while.

My phone buzzed, and I see there was a new message in the group chat. The question was posed...

"What have you done today to get you closer to your goals?"

Unless Jay Jay, *the oldest of the Evans family kids* would help me write a couple articles that I needed to get done, I was at a loss. As my other friends chimed in on all the tasks, they had accomplished that day, I just stared at my phone screen as I shoved another Cheeto into my mouth. While I was sitting around watching TV show re-runs, they were getting busy! They were in action. In that moment, I got up. I turned off the TV, threw my Cheetos bag to the side and went to my computer to get to writing.

My friend circle motivated me to move without directing one audible word my way. I didn't want to be left out of the conversation. I was only the person with nothing to contribute when that question was posed. Watching TV and eating Cheetos would not cut it.

Over the years, I noticed that inner friend groups assist you in thriving all have these five characteristics; let's call them the Top Five. Your inner crew should:

- **Inspire you**
    • They should have qualities you admire, and as a result make you want to work harder.
- **Challenge you**
    • They notice when you are not giving your best and they challenge you to better yourself.

145

- **Listen to you**
  - When you need someone to talk to, they allow you to vent.
- **Have fun with you**
  - You all can have fun and enjoy each other's company.
- **Keep it real with you**
  - They are not afraid to check you when you are wrong, and tell you the truth, in love.

It's key to surround yourself with individuals who hold these characteristics. Why? Because times will get hard to the point quitting looks like an attractive option. But the right crew will help you stay inspired when you get de-motivated and encourage you to get back into the game.

Where to Meet Your Top Five

You may be wondering where to meet people with these characteristics if they are not currently in your life. You never know how and where you might meet someone who becomes a great friend. Check out these resources to get started.

146

Meetup.com

This allows people to come together and create affinity communities. It is simple. You share the topics you are interested in. Then they will search their database and populate events and groups related to it. It is a great place to meet people with common interests as you. They have groups ranging from young entrepreneurs, pregnant ladies and new moms, hip hop introverts, and even a "none of my girlfriends live in this city" group!

Facebook Groups

Who said that you have to get dressed and leave the house to meet people? Check out the various Facebook groups. In the search bar type on the top left of the page, enter your interest area and explore the different groups. You can LIKE a group to be added, unless it is a Closed group. Then you might need to await an okay from the group's Administrator. Once you are a part of the group, be involved in the conversations that take place and post away. Ask questions, post information, and reply to posts within the group. I have seen people be straight forward: *"I am looking for someone to hold me accountable for my goals."* The beauty of the internet is that you can connect with people from all over the world.

Organizations

Alumni associations, fraternities, sororities, service organizations, professional organization, and clubs, are all great places to get plugged into and meet someone for your top five. These groups have people with similar interests and goals as you. Because of the common denominator of being connected to the organization, others are more likely to connect you to people that can help support your dream.

Social Events

Get out and be social. Think: where would people with these five characteristics hang out? Are there networking events, happy hours, conferences, or workshops I need to be attending? I know you may be shy or hate to speak to strangers, but you will be pleasantly surprised how friendly and welcoming individuals who attend social events can be. And if you are deathly afraid to start a conversation with someone, start with asking *"What is it that you do?"* To start with a question to the other that shows your sincere curiosity is usually a great starting place for opening up the lines of communication.

Haters are Everywhere

Unfortunately, everyone you meet will not be throwing you a parade in excitement of you pursuing your dreams. They may be risk-adverse, less exposed, their thinking could be more limited than yours, or they believe that dreams don't come true. Family or friends can also fall into this category, especially if they feel a little threatened by your growth and elevation. Sometimes friends or family want you to remain where you are and not change the nature of your relationship with them. You would think that everyone would automatically be excited that you want to do better, and be better, but this isn't always the case. This can give you mountains of frustration and stress, and even be hurtful. How do you deal when people are discouraging you not to "get on the ride?" How do you deal with others who have never "gotten" on the ride and don't seem to want you to either?

What's weird about haters is that hating doesn't make them an evil person. Who you have the potential

149

to become or who they see you becoming may intimidate them. You may be evolving into a more self-expressed, bold, confident, successful and/or prosperous person, and this creates a different dynamic with you than the one they'd grown accustomed to. Often, what's beneath their naysaying or "*haterade*," is fear of losing the relationships, *as it's been*. When you transform, your hobbies, interests, and behavior will change. And if others around you aren't evolving, it can put a strain on the relationship or change the dynamics. You may even feel you have less and less in common. It can change or even end the relationship.

For example, if you used to always agree with every viewpoint of a certain friend and now you are offering an alternative viewpoint of your own, this can be new. And new can sometimes be perceived as a threat to the status quo. They may not be excited that you no longer go with the flow in every situation. They may love to see you grow, but the unspoken caveat may be: as long as you don't outgrow me.

What Do You Do?

A couple of years ago, my advice would've been simply, cut every one of them haters, *snip, snip, snip, one by one*. Eliminate them all from your life. Now I'll offer you another option. But don't put your scissors up just yet.

When I told my friends that I wanted to be a life coach, a couple of folks didn't support the idea with open arms. That hurt my feelings. These weren't people I was only kind of cool with, nah, these were my ride or dies. These were people I talked to everyday. We were tight like white on rice. I could not, for the life of me, wrap my brain around the fact that they didn't have my back.

This reminds me. Everybody won't be as excited about your dreams as you are, nor should they be. But remember, YOUR dreams are YOUR dreams and not theirs. They did not sign a contract with any obligations to always be enthusiastic and understanding about the things that are important in YOUR life. We must remember, we do it for ourselves and not for the approval or accolades of others.

My friends couldn't understand because from their viewpoints. I reached the goal most were pursuing; landing a job in my field after graduation. So, when I shared my ideas with them, they couldn't grasp the concept. Why would I want to switch gears?

That reminds me, be careful who you share your vision with. We get excited and want to tell the world. However, when we open our mouths, we also open ourselves up to the reactions of others. You're swinging the door open for the opinions of any and everybody. And if the reactions are negative or unsupportive, then it can feel like a blow to the gut. Negative or unsupportive responses have the power to plant seeds of doubt or uncertainty where we initially were confident and sure. Negativity can sway us away from our vision and have us feeling like maybe we're thinking too big.

More importantly, negativity can have us forget that they might be projecting their own fears, concerns or insecurities. Let me say it again - it has nothing to do with you! Instead share your dreams and ideas with those who can relate to them and embrace them - because they have had the experience themselves or have big dreams, too. When I reflected, I realized that my

152

inner circle of friends had no concept of what a life coach did. None of them had a personal life coach, didn't know others that did, and weren't familiar with the profession. It was difficult for them to be as enthusiastic and supportive as I wished. It was outside of their personal experience or ability to relate or understand.

They didn't understand the vision - at least not right away. They shut it down and it made them look like haters. But as my blog and coaching practice unfolded and my words and vision became reality, *they had a change of heart.*

They no longer gave the stale face when I mentioned *The Fear Hurdler.* They even supported it, purchasing merchandise and sharing content with their co-workers. All it took was a little time. Don't be afraid to respectfully communicate with them. Don't say, *"You just don't understand me. Or, I expect you to be happy for me."* Instead, you might say, *"Wow, I thought I would get a different response from you – something a little more positive."* However, let them know that you are working on something that is important to you. Now, if they don't understand that, and they continue to spew negativity, ridicule you, or badmouth your dream, *then* you can bring out the scissors. You can separate yourself from someone without being cruel or vindictive. No need to write a long post on Facebook about how you can't hang with them anymore and how they been talking bad about you doing good. And PLEASE no sub post (not talking directly about them; but everyone knows that you are talking about them). Instead of hanging with them 24/7, you may hang out with them less. You may be in a circle with other people, so you must see them. In conversation don't talk about your dream however. And if this fails adjust and shift your time and attention, you'd been giving them by separating yourself.

No one can do everything by themselves. You may feel you are superwomen or superman; but you will face times when you will want to quit or need a little encouragement. And a great inner circle can do just that. As the saying on social media goes "behind every successful woman, there's a group text hypin' her up."

CHAPTER 7

JUST A 'LIL MORE

"There's always something to suggest that you'll never be who you wanted to be. Your choice is to take it or keep it moving" -Phylicia Rashad

When I decided to expand from only blogging to developing my coaching practice, a friend suggested that I look into SCORE. SCORE is a program created by the government, to offer mentoring services to aspiring entrepreneurs from retired business executives. I went online and gave them information of what I wanted to accomplish and then was paired with a mentor. At our first meeting he asked me "So, how can I help you?" So, I answered "Well, you don't know what you don't know..."

I knew that I had spent endless hours researching business basics but there are things I wouldn't know to even consider. But because he had not only been the president of a financial institution and a consultant; his mentorship could call out the blind spots I didn't know to look for.

This is what I call filling in the gaps. It's the smaller details that are also important that you don't want to overlook, and can make the difference in "the ride." As you look at moving forward into action with your dream, you may realize that you may not know all that is needed to move forward confidently and effectively. A little help from Google and conversations with the people around with a proven track record can drastically change your experience for the better. On this pursuit to your dream, there may be skills, techniques, information, that you will need to acquire first to better maximize your opportunity and ensure your success. I'll share suggested places to start; and as you read, brainstorm ways in which you can fill your gaps in your knowledge, understanding, or even skills.

Fill the Gap

From the goals you created earlier and what you have learned that it takes to reach your dream, now ask yourself: *What are additional skills or knowledge I need to learn?* I call this filling in the gaps. It is like being a new recording artist that just signed to a label. Though you have the talent to sing, the label will continue to develop your voice to become the best artist you have the potential of being. The gaps are the skills, talents, or information that are your growth areas and could be developed.

I always knew public speaking was an ability I wanted to showcase. I never had much of a problem getting in front of an audience and talking their heads off. But I had no idea of how to prepare a captivating presentation. To make it happen, and reach my fullest potential, I needed to fill in the gaps and learn the art of creating a compelling presentation and being organized and impactful in communicating my thoughts to a group. I needed to recognize where I had gaps and then act to UP my skills or my abilities so the gap would be closed. There are three resolves I reached for myself.

Step 1: I don't know everything

When we believe that we have nothing else to learn we fail to seek opportunities to enhance our skills. We never know how one small tweak can become a gain changer.

Step 2: Seek information

157

I had to seek resources by joining Toastmasters International to help me improve on my public speaking skills. Whether it was asking others if they knew which direction to point me in or finding books and articles online regarding the topic.

Step 3: Take what'cha need and act

After gaining information; take the information that is a good fit for you, and relevant, and decide your next steps.

Here is how I put those steps into action.

How to Get it?

Let me get this rant out of the way before we get back into it. *"I don't know what to do,"* is just a poor excuse for you not wanting to get up and do something. Instead of finding the answer, we rely on this excuse to justify us doing nothing. Well my friend *"not knowing"* is an even better reason to go find out! Not knowing is a great reason to get up and get into action. Here are some ideas on how to do so.

Organizations

If I wanted to be a speaker, I had to put on a speaker's shoes and ask: *Where do they hang out? Where do I find speakers? How can I tap into their knowledge?* The first thing I did was holler at my homie Google *(...he always has the answer)*. The results came back telling me about an organization called *Toastmasters International*. It is a group that assists you in improving your public speaking. The name sounded familiar. Duh, Jas. I had seen the flyer on the elevator at work all the time! There was a Toastmasters International club right in my building that met once a week at lunch time. How perfect!

The following week I went to a meeting and it was all that I needed and more. I was provided a speaker's manual with different aids and suggestions that assisted me in putting my speech together. Then you could sign up to give the speech at the meeting. After your speech, you were given feedback on what you did that was great and what you could do to improve. *And here's the icing on the cake* - because I talked to my manager about wanting to give more presentations, my department covered my membership fee! So, I didn't even have

159

to pay out of my pocket! By investing in me in this way, my company was investing in my dreams and didn't even know it. I encourage you to have a conversation with your manager or supervisor, if you have one; you never know they might cover the bill. Communicate how it will benefit the company. It can create a win-win situation.

Mentoring

Let's start with *what is a mentor?* A mentor is a wise and trusted individual with proven mastery in their life and/or career who can serve as a teacher, guide or advisor to you. They may succeed within the industry you desire to pursue or possess traits or character you admire. Before you ask someone to be your mentor, Forbes magazine suggest that you take additional steps.

1. Do your homework on yourself

What would you like to achieve because of this relationship? And what will you be asking your mentor for guidance with?

2. Do your homework on the field

160

What information can you obtain on your own? Don't waste their time if the information you seek can be found from a simple Google search.

3. Do your homework on your potential mentor

Get to know your potential mentor; read their work, visit their website or LinkedIn profile. This will allow you to generate specific questions to ask and maximize your time together.

Now it's time for you to contact them. If this is someone whom you do not know, it will be beneficial to send an email. In this email you should request a 15-minute phone meeting. In the email, you can briefly let them know why you would like them to be your mentor. Keep your email simple and straight to the point. Here is a great example of an email borrowed from the article, *Nine Tips to Land a Great Mentor (Forbes, Nawaz, Sabina, 11 Nov 2015).*

THE ROLLER COASTER EFFECT

Dear Jane,

In 10 years, I aspire to be where you are in your career today: coaching executives and working with leadership teams in the healthcare sector. Based on the testimonials on your website, your methodology has clearly made a big impact. I'd appreciate your help to understand how you entered the healthcare market, so I might begin a similar career path.

Jonathan Baker admires your skills and suggested I contact you. Your insights will add something I can't glean from the research I've done on this sector. I know your time is precious, so I'd like to limit my request to 15 minutes of your time at your convenience. I promise to keep our conversation brief, as I've already done homework on the field and your work. Also, if there's anything I can do to help return the favor, please let me know.

Thanks in advance,
      Jason

      In this example you will notice they were clear on what they were seeking a mentor for, researched the mentor, acknowledge that they have a common connection, and asked for a brief conversation. Be clear about how they could assist them. In this relationship you should expect your mentor to share his/her wisdom and support your growth and development. You want to resist the temptation to consider your mentor a genie in a bottle. We may feel that a mentor will magically make your every wish come true. This is not the case. You want to consider them an essential resource, but not a miracle worker.

It was my last semester in graduate school, and I was still scrambling to secure a job. I was in a desperate position to find what I would do after graduation. So, I saw this as a perfect time to have a meeting with my mentor; or so my mentor could help a sistah out. When we met, I was waiting for the moment when he would drop a revolutionary breakthrough solution on me - the secret sauce to me getting a job ASAP. But instead I heard, *yada yada yada network, yada yada yada thank you cards, yada yada yada.*

I was disappointed.

After our meeting, I agreed in my head I would no longer meet with him because he couldn't give me what I needed. In my mind, I needed him to materialize a job for me – poof! And right now! But I was looking for my mentor to do all the work while I sat back and reaped the benefits.

Tips to consider during your relationship with a mentor:

1. Come prepared with questions and topics you would like to discuss during your meetings.

2. Always be on time to the meeting.

3. Be open to their feedback

4. Complete the assignments they may give you during the meeting or between meetings. If you never act on their suggestions, you are wasting their time.

5. Bring value to the relationship. What is a topic that they may not be as knowledgeable on? (for example: if your mentor is older, they may want to know much about technology and social media). What are creative ways you can thank them for their time? For example, you know that your mentor is working on a book, so you might bring them a nice writing pen in a case.

Remember this is a mentor, not a consultant and not a personal life coach. Life Mentors tend not to charge a fee for their time, while consultants and life coaches do. The mentor will not do the work *for* you; but will provide you valuable information *to* you, that will guide you on the right path.

Learning Never Stops

By the time you have reached your mid-20s, you will realize that much of your life has been spent in an educational setting. From Pre-K to High School to College, and even graduate and postgraduate degrees for some of us can easily take up 18 to 30 years of our lives. When we think of learning, a structured formal environment comes to mind. After the stress, you are school'd out. If you even think about opening another text book, your brain hurts. And just like that, our learning process slows down. We already did our time, right? How dare we do anything more.

Once you're finished with your formal

education, then it's time to be hungry for a new type of learning and self-expansion. Becoming a sponge for information at this point is critical. It allows you to expand on your knowledge base. Books are a great place to gain the information you are seeking. There is bound to be an expert to write on the topic you would like to learn more about. Individuals you might admire like Steve Harvey, Warren Buffet, and Oprah Winfrey have all written books. Though you may not get an opportunity to have a conversation with them, you can gain wisdom from them through their books.

Pick Up a Book

Three years prior to writing this book, you couldn't pay me to read. As soon as the topic was brought up, I had every excuse in the world as to why I wouldn't read a book. Since you have made it to this point in the book, I will not get on my soapbox about people not reading and leave this to be addressed in my blog. Instead, my message to you is to read more. In the last two years alone, I have read over 80 books. These books include everything from research books to self-help and motivational readings. After reading so many books in a relatively short period of time, I will share with you some of my favorites. These books have contributed to:

- shifting my mindset
- a framework on how to run a business
- providing motivation when I felt like quitting
- proof that average people can overcome obstacles and fears to reach great heights of success,
- better money management habits
- me developing a deeper personal relationship with God
- becoming better at networking about how I approach pursing my dreams
- providing me with the tools to believe in myself.

My "Jasamine Must-Read List" includes the following books:

- *The Alchemist* by Paulo Coelho
- *David and Goliath: Underdogs, Misfits, and the Art of Battling Giants* by Malcolm Gladwell
- *You Are a Badass: How to Stop Doubting Your Greatness and Start Living* by Jen Sincero
- *Fervent: A Woman's Battle Plan to Serious, Specific and*

Strategic Prayer by Priscilla Shirer

- *How to Win Friends and Influence People* by Dale Carnegie
- *All the Joy You Can Stand: 101 Sacred Power Principles for Making Joy Real in Your Life* by Debrena Jackson Gandy

There is not a week that goes by that someone does not ask me the infamous question *"Jas, how do you read all of those books?"* The answer is simple. I don't try to find the time, I *make* time because I understand the value of reading. I make sure that every day I carve out at least 45 minutes, five days out of the week, to read. The more that I read, the more insight, understanding, illumination, inspiration and knowledge I acquire.

The reason I strongly encourage others to read is that reading changes your thinking, your perspective, and your perception, and it alters your mind. And when you're thinking, perspective, perception and mindset is changed, it changes your life! Reading gives you a different outlook on topics you wouldn't have thought about previously. Reading is one key that helps you unlock your dreams. Stay informed about industry and world events, too. Start by taking at least ten minutes every day to read, adding on two minutes each day, you will be amazed at what you have learned by the end of the week.

Now that you have the knowledge, when will success come?

CHAPTER 8

QUICK, FAST, AND

IN A HURRY

"You can't prepare in the battle. You have to be battle-tested and ready." – Yvonne Orji

Ever been so hungry that it feels like your stomach is touching your backbone and making noises you never thought it could? You know what you want from Chick fil la. You want a spicy chicken sandwich with no tomato, a medium fry, three BBQ sauces, and a lemonade with no ice *(that's how you get the maximum amount of lemonade)*. But you pull up only to see it is a mad house; the line is wrapped around the building. Just because you are hungry *(desire for more)* and know what you want to eat *(your dreams)*, doesn't mean you get to skip the line *(make it happen overnight)*.

And it's the part of getting on the roller coaster I can't stand: *waiting.* You see the sign for the ride, and it reminds you that from this point the wait time is two hours! Two hours for a five-minute ride! *ARE YOU*

BLEEP BLEEP* MOTHA *BLEEP* KIDDING
ME?!*

    Don't they know I have things to do? But because I
want this, I get into line and "do my time." There are
those who have been talking about the same ride for
months now, then get to this point, see the wait time, and
they get impatient. They decide they don't want it bad
enough to wait, so they turn around. We live in an impatient society. We no longer send postal mail but will
send a text message for a quick reply. Why place a pizza
in the oven when you can pop it in the microwave for a
fraction of the time? And don't get me started. If a wait-
ress takes a long time to bring our food out, we may vow
never to eat there again and may even write a nasty review on Yelp.com.

Give it to Me NOW!

Certain things must be done on the way to fulfilling your
dream - and there's no shortcut, no leapfrogging nor a
proxy. You can't expect to start a business tomorrow
and make the *Forbes 500* list by the end of the week. Similarly, you can't start a new job and become the CEO after one month. You must allow for the "wait" time. That

is part of the process - step by step, getting you closer and closer to your ultimate goal. Though the line for the ride may not seem to move, you will eventually get on the ride if you continue moving forward, step by step.

Take Your Time, Grasshopper

Quick and fast isn't always a beneficial solution. Though it may seem nice in the short run, what good is it if it doesn't last?

Wouldn't it be great to have your dream house built? It is everything that you have ever imagined, just like billionaire music and fashion mogul, P. Diddy's Miami mansion. But the builders you contracted took several shortcuts and completed the mansion in only two weeks. However, the foundation was rushed and wasn't stable. Well, it looked impressive until a storm came and blew it down. Because of the shortcuts and lack of foundation; your dream house didn't last and came tumbling down.

One great thing about "the wait" in line is that it gives a window of time to build a strong foundation by developing your talent and skills. There is value in "the wait." Thank goodness there is a lapse of time between us conceiving a dream and it coming to fulfillment. Often, we need to get ready; we need to get equipped or we need to get prepared to receive it. This can happen during "the wait" time.

You don't want to just arrive at your destiny too fast, and trade off speed and instant gratification and "appearances" for a strong, solid and stable foundation. The quality and durability of the entire structure starts with the solidity of the foundation. You want it to be sustainable and to thrive for years. Just like a house with a strong foundation, it will encounter many storms but will continue to stand strong.

In the last chapter, we talked about the learning factor. It's exciting to explore a field in which you have no experience in. Be a sponge in all that you do! Everything that you face can prepare you for your destiny. Even when the situation isn't ideal.

For example, After I completed undergrad, I had the opportunity to become a Graduate Assistant in the Student Involvement Department at a small University. I had no interest in a career in Student Life, but they would pay for me to complete my Master's program, so I was down for it. In this position, I had to develop and execute several events and workshops based on the needs of the student body. Though I was focused on having a career in sports, that experience helped me develop my own workshops and become comfortable with presenting in front of an audience, skills I still use to this day. What if I refused to do anything but sports after undergrad? I would've missed my chance to develop key skills I use today!

Don't even get me started on the job from hell in sales I mentioned initially. I thought it was useless and only a stepping stone to get me somewhere else inside of the organization. But I learned many key skills and abilities which have assisted me in running my own business: *be persistent, pitch (a sales presentation), focus on the customers' needs, and get comfortable with rejection. (I can't tell you how often people hung up on me - after they cursed me out), how to approach strangers, and how to utilize the client's rejections to sell another product to them.* It didn't mean much to me then, but these soft skills have become the cornerstone of my existence as a business owner.

Reflect on past jobs or internships. *What skills have you learned that you could utilize now?*

We can focus on the outcome and forget the journey to get there. What we coin as an overnight success, includes years of work. Take comedian and actor Kevin Hart. He blew up overnight. What we forget about is all the low-budget, straight–to-DVD movies he starred in "back in the day." And before that, he was grinding to make a name for himself in stand-up comedy clubs. Kevin started stand-up comedy after graduating from high school. It wasn't until 2011 that he broke out as a "star" with his stand-up special *Laugh at my Pain*. It took 13 years of being consistent, persistent, refining and honing his craft, and being ready for the moment that allowed him to become the huge name he is today. He took him 13 years to be an overnight success.

I love to hear Luvvie Ajayi tell her story. Before she became a New York Times Best Selling author of *I'm Judging You,* she was just a blogger giving hilarious commentary on our favorite TV shows. Luvvie had been blogging, not just one, three, or five, but nine years! When she started, she wasn't even the best out there. She says through the years, everyone else gave up and she continued to be consistent and kept doing it. *She out-lasted her competition.* Luvvie used to write reviews on the TV show *Scandal.* Now the creator of the show, Shonda Rhimes, will be creating a show based on Luvvie's book! Talk about a full circle moment! She is reaping the benefits from all her hard and persistent work. *Where would she be if she had given up before her breakthrough moment?*

It opens the door for luck. Yes…. LUCK!

I don't see luck as most do. Let me explain. Many people think of it as something good that falls out of the sky. *Is it really?* Even if you won $100 million, would that be just luck?

I think not!

As the saying goes, luck is when opportunity meets preparation. Think about that. The action of going to a gas station or convenience store and purchasing the ticket and choosing numbers, sets you up for the win. The opportunity is when the jackpot is the right number and they call your number.

Being prepared for the moment increases the chances of that moment being unexpectedly fruitful. When you run into a hiring manager and they ask for your resume *(that you already have updated)* or you encounter someone looking to invest in a cupcake business *(the cupcake business you just completed a business plan for)* …LUCK – opportunity has met preparation!

We miss out because we become caught "with our pants down," *(unprepared)*. You never know when the time will come. *Stay* ready so you don't have to *get* ready.

CHAPTER 9

"I HAVE TO USE THE BATHROOM"

*"Those who are successful overcome their fears
and take action. Those who aren't submit to
their fears and live with regrets." – Jay Z*

Finally, the line is moving. The scenery around you
changes. You can see the ride being loaded. The speakers blare as the attendants give a rundown of safety pre-
cautions: *"Please wait until current riders exit before approaching the ride, once in the seat pull your safety bar down until you
hear a click; then an attendant will be by to double check, blah,
blah, blah…"*

Most of it goes into one ear and out other as you
notice the cart approaching the tracks. Riders are
flushed with colors as they attempt to catch their breath
from such a wild time. It gets your attention. You feel
it in your stomach and in your throat. You can feel your
heart beating through your shirt, your palms begin to experience excessive sweat and your hands start to shake.
The Roller Coaster Effect is in full force.

"I HAVE TO USE THE BATHROOM"

It was over four years ago when I decided to write this book. I was sitting in my cubicle at work when the idea to write a book that showed the parallels and common threads between the journey to achieving your dreams and getting on a roller coaster. Just a few years prior I went to the amusement park Carowinds in Charlotte, NC with my brother and his family. My nephew Donjavious *(we call him DJ)* was around 9 or 10 years old. He didn't want to go to kiddy land with his mom and sister but desired to get on the big rides with me and my brother. DJ was excited. But I noticed his demeanor change the closer we approached our turn to get on. He then started to repeat, *"Aunt Jas, I have to go to the bathroom, I can't hold it any longer."* So, I told him to wait for us to get off the ride and then we would go together.

Once my brother and I got off the ride. I walked over to DJ, *"Ok, now let's go find a bathroom."*

"I don't have to go anymore." DJ said.

I just got played. He was scared, and he was trying to use having to go to the bathroom as his reason for not getting on the ride. Because of that encounter I knew that the "bathroom excuse" my nephew tried to use, and our pursuit of our dreams has commonalities.

In December of 2015, I penned my book outline and got busy, finally. For months I had used a myriad of "I have to use the bathroom" delay tactics. After writing the introduction, I felt I was making progress, so I put it down for a day or two. But then days became weeks, and before I knew it, months had gone by before I picked it up again and started back writing again. My bad. After my vacation, I was back focused and ready to complete this project. After re-reading the first couple of chapters, I hated it. This was my first book and I wanted it to be good, and I felt that what I had completed at this point was garbage. So, I started over.

Maybe I wasn't meant to be an author, I thought. I could've misinterpreted this idea that felt as though it came from God. Instead of a book, maybe it was just supposed to be a Facebook post. I will just go back and focus on my blog. I'm done with this whole being an author thing.

It didn't matter that I put in all this time. It wasn't too late to turn around and act like none of this ever happened. The closer I came to complete my goal, the stronger the urge was to run like hell. I forgot that I had told a couple of people what I was working on. It's like having accountability partners when you didn't even solicit their help. I was over it but their inquiries made me accountable.

"Jas, how's the book coming along?"

My response was always that I had been busy but was working on it. *It was coming along.* That was the biggest lie I had ever told. I didn't even know where my manuscript was. Sometimes I just said I was busy. It was just a sugar-coated excuse to cause others to back off. It was a response that others would believe and they wouldn't challenge me on. They would respond with ok, and keep it moving. I technically was busy; however, but it wasn't busy on my book manuscript. I was busy keeping up on ratchet reality TV and watching *The Breakfast Club* on YouTube, the hip hop morning interview radio show that piqued my interest. I was doing everything but the one thing I KNEW I needed to do. I was scared, damn near frightened. I had a burning desire to complete this book, but my fear took over and placed it last on my priority list.

181

Sugar-Coated Excuses

"Excuses are tools of the incompetent that build monuments of nothingness; those who specialize in them seldom accomplish much else." (Author Unknown). Excuses make us feel we are lawyers building a case for the defense. We find the smallest truth in a story and prove that it is true. Here are some classics *(and I bet some of these are your go-to's):*

- *I don't have time*
- *I can't afford it*
- *I have kids*
- *I don't know anyone in that industry*
- *I've always been that way*
- *I don't have a degree*
- *It will never happen for me*

Let me summarize it for you – these all give you a way out. Let's turn these excuses into tools of empowerment with these steps.

"I HAVE TO USE THE BATHROOM"

Step 1: Awareness

"If you always do what you've always done, you always get what you've always gotten." - Jessie Potter. What makes you stop doing what you've always done? Well, usually when you realize what you're doing ain't working any more, it's an opportunity to become more self-aware. It reminds me of a car with an issue. We don't always know the exact problem right away, but we see the warning lights appear on the dashboard. Each light gives us the heads up that something needs our attention. If the low fuel light appears, then head to the gas station to fill up. The low tire pressure light means put more air in the tires. However, we don't have a dashboard in life that tells us not to use a b. s. excuses. Look to see what is not working well. Have you accomplished what you've set out to do?

Excuses are the barriers that are between where you are and where you want to be. To get there, you must know how to uncover the excuses that have been hiding in the shadows. Excuses are the "fruit" of fear. Of course, first thought isn't to tell people that we are scared as hell to accomplish our dreams. Excuses are a way to discredit ourselves so we can be stagnant instead of moving forward.

You're here -------- Excuse ----------- Dreams

Step 2: Give it another look

I'm not blind by any stretch of the imagination; however, I don't have the best vision in the world. After going to the eye doctor in the 10th grade, I was told that I would have to wear glasses. I can see well without them, but when I put on my glasses, a whole new world appears. I can see everything crystal clear! To have a new vision of your life, you should view your excuses with new lenses.

What would your life look like if these excuses did not exist? Write down what would be happening or occurring if each of your excuses was gone.

_____

_____

_____

_____

_____

_____

———————————————————————

———————————————————————

———————————————————————

———————————————————————

———————————————————————

As self-help author, Dwayne Dyer puts it this way in *Excuses Be Gone*. If you eliminated your excuses,

"...you'd be aligned with a universe that says, "Yes, you can!" and gives you the tools to prove it. You'd have no hesitation or fear that something would be difficult or take too long...you'd happily do rather than explain or complain." Instead of focusing on what you can't do, you will begin to strategize on what you *will* do. Your thought process alters as you move barriers out of your way.

Step 3: Empowerment

It is a beautiful thing to use elements that once held you back as tools to now propel you forward. Not only will you expose the excuse but also overcome the fear. Dr. Wayne shares in *Excuses be Gone* beautiful affirmations to utilize in place of our excuses. Find the one that fits you, write each one on a sticky note and place it somewhere

185

you can see. When you feel the urge to speak excuses, replace them with affirmations.

- Instead of, It will be difficult: I can accomplish any task I set my mind to with ease and comfort

- Instead of, It will take a long time: I have infinite patience for fulfilling my destiny.

- Instead of, I can't afford it: I am connected to an unlimited source of abundance.

- Instead of, No one will help me: The right circumstances and the right people are already here and will show up on time.

- Instead of, I'm not smart enough: I am a creation of the Divine mind; all is perfect, and I am a genius in my own right.

- Instead of, I'm too old (or not old enough): I am an infinite being. The age of my body had no bearing on what I do or who I am

- Instead of, It's too big: I think only about

186

what I can do now. By thinking small, I accomplish great things.

- Instead of, I'm too busy: As I unclutter my life, I free myself to answer the callings of my soul.

- Instead of, I'm too scared: I can accomplish anything I put my mind to, because I know that I am never alone

Don't give in to the urge to use the "bathroom." Remind yourself of the steps: awareness, give it another look, and empower yourself! It's time to get on the ride!

CHAPTER 10

THE POINTOF NO RETURN

*"The biggest adventure you can take is to live
the life of your dreams." – Oprah Winfrey*

Just because you're finally in the seat doesn't mean that
The Roller Coaster Effect is over. The attendant comes
by and double checks your harness then locks in your
row with a loud CLICK of the safety bar. You double,
triple, quadruple check it just in case they missed something - nothing would be worse than to move and your
harness releases. Each attendant throws up a thumb that
their section is good to go, the conductor then com-
municates that we are good to go and finally we may enjoy the ride. As the ride creeps out of the tunnel, you
can't believe that it's finally actually happening. You got
on the ride! And once you realize that it really about to
happen, you begin to panic.

I have lost my damn mind!

What the hell is wrong with me?

THE POINT OF NO RETURN

Is there still time to get off!

You can seem to turn into an extra in a super-hero movie and thoughts of escaping enter your mind. As the ride creeps up the first steep rollercoaster hill you notice the metal staircase to the right. If you can only use your laser beam powers to release you from your harness, do a backflip and land on the steps, walk down and wait for all your friends at the end of the ride!

Then you remember that you don't have super-powers. *What if I just frantically wave my hands so that the attendants can see me, or yell? I'm sure they will stop the ride and allow me to get off. There is still time! No, I can't do that. Yes, I can. No, I can't.* Our minds can be caught in a back and forth debate. After this confrontation in your head, you look to see you are too far gone at this point, it's really going to happen. There's no turning back.

You can feel like your death awaits, but you realize that you just got to face it, head on. So, you close your eyes *(to avoid getting more spooked)* and pray as if your life depended on it. But it does, because this is it, it is the end; or at least it feels like it. Then you feel conflicted. Though your eyes are closed, it is freaking you

189

out because you don't know what's happening. So now you look like a weirdo, opening and closing your eyes repeatedly because you become conflicted on whether you should look or not.

As your eyes open, you noticed that it looks like a new world up here, you can not only see the entire park, but the whole city. Holy Smokes! It's a view you've never seen before, an experience you've never had before, and a feeling you have never felt before. Wow! It's a beautiful sight. It can freak you out though because you are up so high.

I wonder if this is how LeBron feels when the game is tied and there are only five seconds left. The Coach calls a timeout just to draw up a special play, and he wants LeBron to take the last shot. I mean, he is one of the greatest basketball players of our time. What is going through LeBron's head when he leaves the huddle? Does he have the same thoughts that we are having on this roller coaster? This scenario can go two ways; make the shot and win the game or miss it and deal with the disappointment and the incessant media questions afterwards. No matter the hesitation that he may experience; he takes the shot. A few times he has missed, but how often has he sunk the winning shot and created an historic end? It is one reason he is a living basketball legend - he would take the shot! Do the same and be ready to take the shot. When worried about the task at hand, take the chance and take the shot. It could secure you the win in your own life.

The Infamous Pause

The cart is moving at such a snail's pace that you hear every click, click, click of the pulley. The moment that has felt like forever is finally here. The line of carts if finally, at the apex of the first BIG hill. But before the lever is released and gravity takes its reign of control, you take a deep breath to brace yourself. *Click....click...click...* Then you hear nothing. You're no longer moving - the ride has stopped. Everyone looks around at each other in curiosity: there is an unexpected pause in the movement of the carts that gets everyone's attention.

At this point you may be expecting to be free falling down the first hill but first there is the pause. The same may happen with your launch. You release the blog or business and you hear only crickets. There may be a pause. Don't be tempted to throw it all away. As you work towards fulfilling your vision, during a pause is a great time to reflect and review. *What is working? What could be improved? What small tweaks need to be made?*

Look at Oprah, for example. She was told that she didn't belong in front of the camera. If she would've packed her bags and went home, I wouldn't be watching Super Soul Sundays. Don't be so easy to give up just because you face a struggle. There were several "pauses" along the way to her becoming a billionaire and a leading media icon.

Because before you know it, after the pause at the crest of the hill you're descending from over 100ft up, going 70mph. Your cheeks flap in the air like a dog sticking its head out the car window. By this time your stomach is in your throat. The frightening thoughts that led up to this moment disappear as it becomes the most exhilarating moment in your life. *It is thrilling!*

I remember when this pause happened for me as a blogger. I felt that I was stuck on top of the hill for a while, and ready to move into momentum. After the initial launch of my blog, I was only writing posts for

192

myself. Well, the analytics seemed to also confirm that I was one of the only ones reading my blog. *What was I still doing it for?* I know it had only been two months, but I felt discouraged. But right before I decided to stop blogging, I had forgotten that I had submitted a request to be a contributor for a popular motivational site. It was the first site outside of my own that I would be a contributor for. So, I wanted to make an "awesome sauce" introduction, but as I tried to think of topics. I was stumped!

I was sitting at my part-time job brainstorming blog ideas for this other site when someone asked me about a book, I was currently reading. I know it might sound corny, but in response to the question, I was inspired to create a book list that folks should read. Right there on the spot. I looked through my library and found the top ten books I believed every black woman should read. Once I completed the list, I was proud of what I had put together. So, I submitted my Top Ten finished product and waited for the notification that the article was successfully published. There it was live and in living color. I wrote a short caption and shared it with my network. Much to my delight and surprise, when I logged on to Facebook, the post had been shared on social media by readers hundreds of times. And when I visited the website at the end of the week, I discovered that it had been shared over 40k! Wow!

I had to refresh my screen several times because I thought there was a glitch in the system. I thought this was some type of mistake. If that wasn't icing on the cake, when on my way to Bible Study the following week, my phone sent me an email alert. I figured that it was probably just a store sending me coupons and sale notifications - the same ole same ole. But it was from one of the authors of a book that I had featured, she wanted to discuss working with her on a project! Mind.... BLOWN! It allowed me to believe in myself and my abilities.

Before I felt that I was just talking to myself and what I had to say didn't have value but seeing the reaction of the readers and how it moved them to read more and even start book clubs, I got a confidence boost in my abilities to write and share valuable content. Once people read the article, they clicked the link to my site and became followers of *The Fear Hurdler*. I saw my site viewership increase by 500%. I haven't looked back

THE POINT OF NO RETURN

since. But what if I would've given up the first time? What if after my "pause" of little readership of my blog for the first couple of months I would have given up, and thrown in the towel because I didn't see the results I expected?

I know one thing - I wouldn't be sitting here talking to you right now and you certainly wouldn't have this book that you're reading! So, the next question is - what do you do once you gain momentum? Let's talk about that.

Maximizing the Moment

The speed is crazy fast, it only slows down for a moment then snatches your wig. Out of nowhere it hits full speed. Just look at certain reality TV stars. Many have been able to capitalize on this very concept.

Let's take Nene Leaks of *The Real Housewives of Atlanta*, one of my favorite ratchet reality shows on Bravo. With her wittiness and clever sayings, she became the face of the franchise. Though the show's ratings were through the roof, she decided to diversify and pursue other opportunities. She started with acting and grabbing a role on the hit show *Glee*, then starring in the Broadway play *Cinderella*. And it didn't stop there. She now headlines her own comedy tour. Nene's career was already doing well, but she took it to the next level. She didn't rest on her laurels. What if she would've stayed complacent, in her comfort zone, and they booted her off? She would have had all her eggs in the Bravo TV basket. But instead, she pursued other opportunities even though the "housewives" show was a blockbuster. She kept her eye on the bigger picture and make key decisions to expand her brand as an actress and entertainer.

Social media influencers are following the same formula. DC Fly was once just a funny guy on Instagram cracking jokes and telling everybody to *"Briiinnnng dat ass heeerree, Boi!"* Now when you turn on the TV or the movies you will see him on *Nick Cannon's Wild'n Out, New Edition's Biopic, and "Almost Christmas,".* Capitalize on opportunities and use them as a spring board to launch higher or expand. I'm not saying don't have deep gratitude for where you are and the successes you may achieved. I'm simply saying, don't get complacent. Instead think strategically and use it as leverage to springboard you to your next level.

As the blog continued to take off, it was time for me to keep the momentum and expand my brand. A fellow blogger suggested that I do a podcast. I thought that would-be dope. I love to talk and besides, I listened to them all day. And I knew that my audience also had time during their commute or during their workday to listen. I started a podcast entitled *"The Perfectly Imperfect Grind"* where I interviewed entrepreneurs about their journey of starting and thriving in business. The show not only inspired my audience but also showed me that I am a really good interviewer. My mentor even coined me as "the Millennial Oprah" after hearing an episode because I was authentic but also get the story out. That talent allowed me to become comfortable in not only speaking (which I spoke of earlier developing) but releasing more videos and starting a YouTube channel!

Building relationships are another key element in gaining momentum. One value I have found to be VERY USEFUL is to always carry myself professionally and treat people with respect. Be humble and have grace. Treat everyone from the intern to those in the C-Suite (the top senior executives for an organization) with respect. Even if they don't remember a name, people always remember how you treat them and made them feel.

Appreciate the Journey

Have you even been so focused on driving to work that once you get there you don't remember the details of how you got there? The entire journey to work can be a blur and you can also feel like you've been teleported. You can be on auto-pilot. And that's the mindset we can fall into on our journey - getting to our destination with no idea of how we got there. Respect the journey. Be present to the journey – every step of it. The lessons you learn along the way enrich you and will come in handy as you continue to progress and grow.

I once worked in sales. It wasn't the ideal job but more of a stepping stone. I knew where I wanted to be, however I had to make ends meet, and being a part of the organization could equip me with additional opportunities. I completed several sales trainings with the best in the industry. But if I forgot my journey, and my bigger dream, I would never have ever moved beyond that sales position and then be able to use that information I learned while there. There were some important tools I used along the way.

Journaling is a tool and a practice that allows you to reflect and can help you live in the moment. It is a positive practice to incorporate into your life and your success journey. Journaling is a way to document your journey, make note of the learnings, the insights, the challenges, and how you overcame them. Journaling can also be a place to capture your creative thoughts, bright ideas, goals and objectives, and your plans. Journaling can give you a place to chronicle and archive the journey, and come to more deeply appreciate what you've conquered, where you've triumphed, and where you persevered. You can see the progress in writing first hand and come to more greatly appreciate every step of your journey. It's helpful to use prompts to get our "journaling juices" flowing. These journal prompts will allow you to gain perspective on your situation and clarify your thoughts. Here are some prompts to help get you started.

- *Dear Future Self, I want you to know.......*
- *Dear God...*
- *I'm currently struggling with......*
- *This week, I accomplished…....*

- *Ten years from now, my heart's desire is......*
- *I'm holding myself back by..........*
- *To me, success, means.......*
- *Envision your dream life. My day consists of.......*
- *I'm grateful for.......*

It is a beautiful thing to look back on your journal entries and receive glimpses into your thinking and mindset.

Journaling will also allow you to reflect on what you overcame. When new challenges present itself, we sometimes catch amnesia. So, we must reflect on the past obstacles to remind us of the strength that we have to beat fear. And once we do, we can reach back and help someone else realize that they have what it takes to overcome fear.

CHAPTER 11

SHOUT IT FROM THE

MOUNTAIN TOP

"Reach out and touch somebody's hand. Make this world a better place, if you can." – Diana Ross

The ride slow down as we return to the place where we started. Your hair is tousled; your voice is hoarse from all the screaming; and your heart is thumping. You and your crew reach over the rows to fist bump each other and exchange smiles of accomplishments; *"How did you like it?"* The reply is, *"That was DOPE!"* The ride comes to a halt and the safety bar is released as the instructions to exit are given. As you glance behind you, to those next in line for the ride, you see a line of glossy-eyed folks looking as though death is waiting for them. Just moments ago, that was you - fearful of the one experience that changed your life forever. But as you look, all you want to do is give them a hug and tell them to just do it, it won't be so bad, and that it will all be worth it.

THE ROLLER COASTER EFFECT

My crew is hyped, skipping down the exit ramp still in a daze from the high. Everyone recaps their favorite moments. The comments:

"The first drop was something serious…"

"I thought we were going to fall in the lake!"

"Every time it felt like it was going to end, it started all over again."

With the hills, twist and turns, the pauses, "the wait," the negative self-talk you had to overcome while standing in line, you made it and you couldn't be prouder of yourself in this moment. You have accomplished your goal; successfully launched the business, rocking it out at your dream job, or flourishing with offering your idea out into the world. The fate that once seemed impossible is now real life. Isn't that something? It's great to work hard and live and breathe what you thought would only be a distant dream. And because you may still be in your "waiting-in-line phase" or your "pause phase" as you finish this book, it's okay. Here's what I want you to remember: IT WILL BE ONE OF THE MOST EXHILIRATING FEELINGS THAT YOU

HAVE EVER EXPERIENCED! All the hard work you are putting in now will pay off; and then you can blast a song of victory that gets you hyped and turned up.

Remember: don't be selfish with your journey – also encourage someone else.

Reach Back

Remember all the people you encountered on your way to getting on the ride? The friends who were there, mentors that guided you along the way, and the random folks who gave you a chance? Don't become one of those I-made-it-on-my-own kinda folks. Where would you be without them, and without the growing and stretching experiences? You didn't do this alone. None of us do. Now it is not only your duty to share your story but to be there for others.

I believe in karma (the more good that you do the more good things happen for you. The more bad, sneaky underhanded things you do, the same bad things will come back around to you). So, don't get too high and mighty on your horse. You can get knocked down. Remember, pride comes before the fall. The more you

THE ROLLER COASTER EFFECT

give the world, as a form of reciprocity and gratitude, and paying it forward, the more it circulates around to give back to you. So, it creates a circle of win-win.

It's like tithing - giving God ten percent of your income. I will never forget the time I was sitting in church and literally had about $5.00 to my name. I felt the urge to put it into the offering basket, so I followed the feeling and did it. Monday when I checked my mailbox, I had received a NICE check from a legal matter for which I did not know that I would be given any reimbursements. When you do good things, the energy from the action has a way of circulating back to find you. It says so much about your character, you know the part of you that tells what type of person you are. Don't be afraid to be a part of making someone else's dreams come true.

FINAL WORDS

"It's been a long, a long time coming
but I know a change gonna come, oh yes it
will" - Sam Cook

Well my friend, YOU DID IT! I am so proud of you!! I hope that you are "there" or well on your way. As we reach the final words of this book, I want to remind you that success is a journey. For all the excitement, it also has its share of trials and hardships. No matter what life throws at you, remember to follow the principles outlined in this book.

We were all placed on Earth for a purpose that is bigger than us. I don't want this book to make you feel good and only leave you inspired. Trust me, after reading 80 books in a year, I know this all too well. But when I implemented and took action on the information, my life took a DRASTIC change.

The blog is no longer just a blog, but a business. I still love to write, but on the website, I now offer coaching packages to assist others to push past fear in pursuit of their dreams, motivational apparel, my YouTube channel (Fear and Faith) where I house my video series "If Scripture was in the Urban Dictionary," and speaking at events. Whew Chile, yes, a lot is going on, and a lot of hard work, but I am LOVING EVERY MINUTE OF IT!

When reaching this portion of the book, my editor instructed me to write about how I was feeling after confronting my fears. I wracked my brain for days, because I couldn't find the words. I felt it but couldn't articulate it. The only word that came close to describing it was freedom. When I encountered fear, I was left with two choices: to be held as a prisoner behind bars wishing I could be free or follow my heart on a path to my dreams. When I followed my heart, I took on a journey that showed me a new strength and confidence that I didn't realize that I possessed. I was now accomplishing goals that once would scare me to death by just thinking of it. This feeling of freedom gave me a new perspective that I could accomplish anything - my dreams weren't a distant fantasy but a close reality. Now I let my fears fuel me. When I sense it in my presence, I get excited; because I know that something great is waiting for me on

FINAL WORDS

the other side of fear.

No dream is out of your reach!

Buckle up, it's time for YOU to get on the ride of your life!

ACKNOWLEDGEMENTS

There are so many people that helped me turn my idea into this great book. First, I have to say that I am so grateful that God chose me to carry this message. He continues to shock me in how he works through me to fulfill my purpose. To the Hill clan, my mama, brothers Ju and Jeremy, aunts, uncles, cousins, nieces, and nephew; thank y'all for always being my biggest cheerleaders in everything that I do. And a special shout out to Ju and Charmaine for reminding me at every moment that I needed to start my blog. I was annoyed at the time but now I'm thankful that you both never gave up on getting me to chase my dream. To Daphnie, Keiona, Dymond, Cherrelle, Jasmine Ford, Sophia, Isis, and Anika y'all are the best friends/sorors a gal could ask for! Thank you for always being willing an open ear to me talking about this book and giving your insight and feedback. Mrs. Debrena, my editor. You are the truth! You made me a better writer throughout this process. Thank you for getting this book tight and teaching me along the way. Ana, you brought my book title to life with the cover art, thank you! To my clients and readers of The Fear Hurdler, I don't have the words to express my gratitude. Thank you all for allowing me to live my purpose daily. For anyone I may have missed, charge it to my head and not my heart!

ABOUT THE AUTHOR

Jasamine Hill is a Life Coach, blogger and the Founder of The Fear Hurdler- a brand dedicated to teaching Women to defeat fear and do the work that they love. After overcoming a few fears of her own, Jasamine recognized how her God-given talents and transitioned from Corporate America into a wealth of entrepreneurial opportunities.

Jasamine began her coaching business shortly after getting her coaching certification in 2015. Her willingness to help others see their potential led her to begin capturing unique clientele that sought to identify their self-imposed limitations and barriers to progress.

To date, Jasamine has written captivating articles that have been featured on LifeHack.org, Blavity, and 21ninety just to name a few. In between working actively working her brand, you may find her on the campus of Johnson C. Smith University as an adjunct professor in the Department of Health and Human Performance. Jasamine is a renowned speaker and member of Toastmasters International, the International Coaching

Federation, and Delta Sigma Theta Sorority, Inc.

When Jasamine isn't leading others to FearLESSness, you can find her at Chick fil A eating a Spicy chicken sandwich, with three BBQ sauces, and sipping a lemonade with light ice (because that is how you get more juice).

For speaking or media inquiries contact Jasamine at: info@TheFearHurdler.com

You may also connect with her the following ways:

Website: www.TheFearHurdler.com

Email: Jasamine@TheFearHurdler

Instagram: @TheFearHurdler

Twitter: @TheFearHurdler

Facebook: www.Facebook.com/TheFearHurdler